Bitches with Problems

Bitches with Problems

Bridget Ryan

Hidden Brook Press

First Edition

Hidden Brook Press
www.HiddenBrookPress.com
writers@HiddenBrookPress.com

Copyright © 2017 Hidden Brook Press
Copyright © 2017 Maureen Gallagher

All rights revert to the author. All rights for book, layout and design remain with Hidden Brook Press. No part of this book may be reproduced except by a reviewer who may quote brief passages in a review. The use of any part of this publication reproduced, transmitted in any form or by any means, electronic, mechanical, photocopied, recorded or otherwise stored in a retrieval system without prior written consent of the publisher is an infringement of the copyright law.

Bitches with Problems
by Bridget Ryan

Editors – David Bateman, Ruth Zuchter
Layout and Design – Richard M. Grove
Cover Design – Richard M. Grove
Illustrations – Darren Emonds
Cover Art – William McCarthy

Printed and bound in Canada
Typeset in Garamond
Printed and bound in USA
Distributed in USA by Ingram,
in Canada by Hidden Brook Distribution

Library and Archives Canada Cataloguing in Publication

Ryan, Bridget, author
    Bitches with problems / Bridget Ryan. -- First edition.

Poems and short stories.
ISBN 978-1-927725-48-1 (softcover)

    I. Title.

PS8635.Y343B58 2017   C818'.609   C2017-900606-1

The only ones for me are the mad ones, the ones who are mad to live, mad to talk, mad to be saved, desirous of everything at the same time, the ones who never yawn or say a commonplace thing, but burn, burn, burn, like fabulous yellow roman candles exploding like spiders across the stars.

– Jack Kerouac, On the Road

*Dedicated to
Kevin Jake*

Contents

Introduction – *p. xii*

The Warm Up – *p. 1*

Five Bitches in a Pack
    1. Bridget (Jet) – *p. 6*
    2. Mia – *p. 7*
    3. Gabrielle – *p. 10*
    4. Susan – *p. 11*
    5. Laura – *p. 12*

Abars – *p. 14*
The Thinker – *p. 17*
"White Kids on Dope" – *p. 19*
A Bette Davis Greeting – *p. 20*
Cottage 13 – *p. 25*
Patsy Cline Crazy – *p. 29*
Moths, Champagne & Stars – *p. 31*
Nancy – *p. 34*
Cottage Drama – *p. 37*
Me and Slyvia – *p. 44*
Wishing, Praying – *p. 45*

True Stories, False Teeth
    1. groceries – *p. 48*
    2. teeth – p. 51

Dianna – *p. 55*
Dr. Walker – *p. 60*

Two Bitches – One Cottage
    1. Judith – *p. 65*
    2. Caroline – p. 66

Tennis Tales – Love Fifteen
- 1. murder city/murder ball – *p. 69*
- 2. my first racquet – *p. 72*
- 3. love one lots – *p. 78*

Bad & Sad – *p. 87*
Anne – *p. 89*
Weekends – *p. 95*
Marijuana – *p. 97*

The Centres – One Day's Journey Into…
- 1. Prelude – *p. 102*
- 2. Get me outta here – *p. 108*
- 3. North Bay Treatment Centre – *p. 109*
- 4. Sanderson Treatment Centre – Toronto – *p. 115*
- 5. Oshawa Treatment Cenre – *p. 121*
- 6. Ohio – Jackson Hill Treatment Centre – *p. 124*
- 7. The Treehouse Treatment Centre – Guelph – *p. 126*

Epilogue – Love is a Drug – *p. 131*
           The Horror – *p. 134*

The Stories…
- Panic – *p. 144*
- Locomotion – *p. 146*
- The Man Is Naked – *p. 152*
- Shoveling Shit – *p. 156*
- The Homecoming – *p. 160*
- Mr. Sexy – *p. 163*
- Game Over – *p. 166*
- Epiphany – *p. 169*

Author Bio Note – *p. 173*

Introduction

Bridget Ryan is a true Renaissance woman hell bent on getting her story out there. With all the pitfalls, the glory, and a variety of riotous leaps into a young life of sex, drugs and rock 'n' roll, she tells the tale of a strong woman who simultaneously resists and embraces the "bitches with problems" scenario as a kind of toxic masculine construct, that the women she meets and the woman she becomes must acknowledge, live through, and rise above. This strategy becomes a way of coping, marked vigorously with an ongoing and relentlessly positive mode of survival. Her first person account takes ownership over all of the trials, tribulations, traumas, and elations that have challenged her and contributed to the diverse and varied ways in which she recounts the rocky journey she has taken, and survived.

In poetic form, as well as a very direct, at times conversational style, her words follow an autobiographical route that brings the reader into a present where she both critiques and cherishes the memories – the books the boys the booze and the all around debauchery – as she moves seamlessly from her teens into adulthood, all the time confronting a life of romance, rebound, and recovery.

The poems and stories that make up this overall sequential journey, include a cast of characters, men and women, who are distinguished by the manner in which the speaker finds rich and layered ways of describing both the good, the bad and the truly bizarre in a series of remembered narrative moments. Nancy, in a see-through negligee, and fond of Scrabble, wanders through rarified public spaces and simultaneously enchants, befriends, and bewilders the narrator who sees a profoundly unique personality amidst the chaos of Nancy's fractured identity.

There are helium happy dentists, Ferris Wheels, suave English dudes, and the tableau-like enchantment of 'five bitches in a pack' as they struggle with and celebrate identities that long to be recognized beyond the objectifying cultural practices that misconstrue female power and agency as bitchiness and bad behaviour.

Bridget Ryan recalls stories from her life that entertain, educate, and ultimately help to purge, soothe, and celebrate survival as the writer and the reader move through forms of written trauma that many can relate to and learn from.

The Warm Up

at seven
reading newspapers – serial novels
Nancy Drew boned by *Hardy Boys*
head buried in books

no family bonds – them downstairs
living their lives
me in my room in fantasy worlds
left books behind long enough to get to school to read

an accidental child
unplanned babies always get the short end
from parents too old to start again
books boys later booze parented me

our home a skeleton of love
like all the houses that would follow
all the playing spaces – dive bars cheap cars
concerts hotels and back seat bands to follow

but before all the grownup stuff begins
still happy alone at home – false contentment
playing tennis in the summer
discovering *Catcher in the Rye* at twelve

then Dorothy Parker
loving her faux suicide ode
all the Algonquin writers
devouring Salinger, Kerouac, Burroughs and Ginsberg

dove into that sacred 'Zen On the Road' wave of realism
always preferring true stories to fiction –
even at the movies
hitting puberty head-on

book crazy boy crazy

reading in my room knocking tennis balls
over and over again at Herman High
playing tennis, soccer or baseball
swimming and running constantly

always on the move
with Dorothy – some wild round table
always there somehow
behind me urging me on

> *Acids stain you;*
> *And drugs cause cramp.*
> *Guns aren't lawful;*
> *Nooses give;*
> *Gas smells awful;*
> *You might as well live.*

> *Dorothy Parker*

always drawn to dark-haired boys
my boy-optic vision of coal-haired Kerouac
blond guys disappearing on my horizon
no fair-haired surfer boys through my radar

eyes glazed over and zoom
focused on someone who was
dark and handsome
I didn't care what he was like

all about looks then
later, maturity reigned
the person inside became important
smart and funny – engage and intrigue me

enrage and mistreat me
my mantra defeats me – a mascot to keep me in line
I learned it all at home
took it all the way into adulthood

broke my first heart at seventeen
he was sweet softly naive
lost my virginity to him
he turned up at my front door

said, "I'll marry you"

so "out there" to "go all the way"
not what Catholic girls
in private school uniforms
were all about

drove around in my soon-to-be heartbroken
boyfriend's little Falcon
listening to The Doors, Janis Joplin
Crosby, Stills, Nash and Young

at home, I would fall asleep my radio tuned to WABX Detroit
best radio station in the world
sang along with Marvin Gaye, The Temptations,
    Smokey Robinson
The Supremes, Stevie Wonder, B.B. King,
    Aretha Franklin, The Four Tops

sweet soul music

I was different and too young to be a hippie…
    more of a beatnik
dressed in black with pointy-toed boots
most people were wild about
    The Rolling Stones and The Beatles
but I had gone through all that

and was looking for alternative forms

being in Windsor
across the water from Detroit
the perfect spot for a young girl
music exploding in the late sixties and the seventies

all the while I was
safe at home
as my eldest brother
did his third tour of duty

my American brother in Vietnam
signs up with the Marines
at sixteen – lies about his age – wanted to get away

from our very stern dad – not the loving Daddy
        we needed him to be
every time my mouth opened he would yell
        before I spoke

"Jesus, Mary, and Joseph, for the love of God,
        would you just shut up!"

Five Bitches In A Pack

1. Bridget (Jet)

the leader of the pack – that old song
but we were girls
in tennis clothes

high school uniforms
sweaters with buttons
pinks and pastels

on our way to hell
in small cars in pursuit of
big boys playing little men

love 15
love 30
love lost
love won

2. *Mia*

while being pounded on the tennis court
my best friend, Mia
had a great time

smoking pot and taking wild, crazy rides
in the county at night
she had a new boyfriend
        Neal – we called him "the pusher man"

the savage and uncivilized
part of my psyche
chained to the stuffy world

of tennis for so long
another nature beckoned
which craved excitement

and yearned to be free

escape was what I wanted
sick of competition
in the tennis world – little did I know
battle beyond the court would be

just as harsh
but it was a helluva lot more fun – at first
Mia had been my best friend since grade nine

we were drawn to each other
because we were both a little docile
a little introverted

and I like
        (a little docile – a little introverted)

and I love to think, a little deep
we were the same size, which is important
to best friends

> like Cathy and Patty
> walked alike talked alike…
> what a crazy pair
> we could trade clothes

Mia, a sweet and gentle girl
when she wore her cheerleading outfit
(even stoned on acid) – the whole
school loved her

she was loyal and stuck by my side
spent every free moment together
discussing issues of great
importance…to us – we talked about it all

but boys were our number one topic
and where and how to get drugs
and how much money we had to get drugs
and what nights we were going to do the drugs

every Tuesday we had our meeting in the cafeteria
the five of us deciding
where when what how who do we ask
about drugs, about boys,
        about boys with drugs about drugs and boys

still trapped in Windsor – Catholic girls
clocking Ian at an Alice Cooper concert
at Walkerville, an uptown school
I liked him a lot and so

we infiltrated the hip guys group
never looking back
at our own high school
eating mushrooms and smoking hash

Mia still involved with "the pusher man"
we got all our drugs from him
we were the second tier in the
drug world of our high school

first tier were wealthy girls chipping heroin at sixteen

of the five girls I ran with
they all went off
to do normal things and married
doctors lawyers, business chiefs

except me

3. Gabrielle

by the end of grade ten
we had made a few
more friends who
shared our sensibilities

Gabrielle – so exceptionally
endowed, all the boys
would flock around
at football games and

everywhere we went
they never had a chance
she was too smart
to fall for it

indifferent to the attention she received
she would laugh and say to me,

If we could only put your head
on my body, we could storm Hollywood.
We could make it all the way to the top, baby!

she had an X-rated body
but didn't like it
when I stood at the end of the hallway at school
and called her 38, she hid behind her locker door

sensible and grounded
not one to take any risks
or chances with chancers
if too high she'd go home

we took that walk on the wild side
she stayed on the safe side

4. Susan

tall
large breasts
gorgeous

boys crazy about her
funniest thing I saw her do
brought a knee-high guy
to our high school dance

Susan – politically astute – resident intellectual
the third member of our little group
denizen cynic and an unforgiving misanthrope
she kept us grounded with her extended stream

of wickedly pessimistic observations
about our insipid private Catholic school
our stupid madras plaid uniforms
those uniforms bore the brunt

of her disdain – and most of her most caustic remarks
they were wool and had to reach below our knees
it was torture wearing those
godforsaken kilts in hot weather

our parents forced us to attend private
school and shelled out good money
that we might enjoy the oppressive privilege
little did they know

God couldn't help us now

5. *Laura*

the fifth and final
component of our secret circle
the most romantic of us all
so slender (much to my chagrin)

beautiful and oh, so fragile
had a bad habit of constantly falling madly
in love – invariably crying
over one guy or another

she could be intense

we just tried
to sustain her through
every affair of her young and
delicate heart

she loved to love
but seemed happiest
when she was miserable

so there we were:

      1 the bookish athlete
      2 the cute cheerleader
      3 the buxom bombshell
      4 the skeptic
      5 our fragile little love addict

all dressed in our appalling Catholic uniforms
a group most unlikely to infiltrate
the dark underworld of sex, drugs and rock'n'roll

God's plan somehow brought us all together
as we developed an intense need
to explore the forbidden

only God couldn't save us now

Abars

We loved sneaking into Abars, on the water,
where the big boys and girls played:

a somewhat seductive seedy bar
a swaggering shambling saloon
the original rickety wooden hotel
kneeling on the grimy banks of the Detroit River

a honky-tonk bar!
the perfect dive bar with
pickled eggs and beef jerky
and booming jukebox

filled with great music
we riverside voyageurs
on hot summer nights
underage and undercover

we primped and wore lip gloss
white jeans with serious belts
trying to break the Age 18 law
we would connive and pass slack doormen

edging through to the back to regroup
sitting at the big round table near the band
the table on the dance floor and the one
furthest from the bar

an untouchable dream
for uncarded youth
but Abars was the happening
place, with all the cool bands

and all the cool guys

scoping the bar for
older siblings
who would surely escort us out
by our ears

we danced in the humid secrecy of youth
daring to have lived lives
too young
too soon

The Thinker

The Thinker

driving through the Windsor-Detroit tunnel
the river overhead
at eighteen
always a little afraid

making that sharp right turn
into the bad part of town
all the bars and the music we craved
you turn left you went into

less dicey parts
tame zones – like home

a big repro sculpture of Rodin's *The Thinker*
at the crossroads between that fork in the road
stop for a split second and think
was it the right thing for me to do?

always making that hard right turn
in the little Volkswagen Beetle Mum bought me on
my sixteenth birthday
painted electric blue by my brother

everyone knew where I was in that bright-blue Bug

> *"Saw you at Kentucky Fried eating all that crap,
> with your little Bug in the parking lot"*

but one time noticing giant green-painted footsteps
from the base of the sculpture all the way
to another sculpture of a naked woman
illuminated across the avenue

with all the promise of the turns
we take when the choices
seem to sit like stone
waiting for us to choose

like that big bronze guy sitting there
finally made up his mind
got up and stomped over to her
to chat about life

about sitting there sitting all the time
never moving only thinking
I never thought that long
just made the hard right turn, thinking

"I guess he finally decided"

"White Kids on Dope"

To me, punk rock is the freedom to create, freedom to be successful, freedom to not be successful, freedom to be who you are. It's freedom.
  — *Patti Smith*

we burst across the border
into the lethal streets of Detroit
a punk bar called Bookies
at 6 Mile and Woodward

dangerous territory but we didn't care.
it was run by transvestites
with a long beautiful bar that ran
from the front to the back

huge men dressed as women served us our drinks

once Patti Smith was there dancing by herself
another night Keith Richards stood at the bar
the Stones had played Detroit
all that fame laid out before me – straight to my head

Rod Stewart, Tina Turner, Iggy Pop, David Bowie
Lou Reed, Pete Seeger, Albert King
there was a song I remember called

"White Kids on Dope"

that became a prophesy…

A Bette Davis Greeting

none of us there
had dealt with life very well
some less than others
the day I arrived, the rain, heavy and dark

long drive
into the estate
enough to scare me
into turning back

felt like we
were just driving
along a quaint country road
never seeming to end

becoming more ominous – intimidating
the further we drove
like opening credits

for the gothic thriller my life had become
driven by imagination and addiction
driven along through miles
and miles of thick forest

when finally we found the place
dark and forbidding
half expecting to see bats flying
out of the belfry

lightning flashing exploding in the sky

Bette Davis, greeting me at the door
(the older Bette Davis, face all wrinkled
but beautiful in a ghastly sort of way)

"Hello. We've been expecting you. Come right in."
no Bette Davis, not even a cheap knockoff,
just some weird old broad in a uniform
welcoming me to the most unwelcoming place

her head about to disappear inside
her smoke-framed mouth
smoking furiously
with a sinister smile and the famous "What a dump!"

dripping from
her creased red lipstick
running like webbed streams through her upper lip
becoming deep rouge rivers to her nostrils

Cottage 13 and surrounding environs: a real dump

a great, big, beautiful dump
the romantic beauty of the lovely, leafy laneway
turning into a miles-long ordeal
trying to imagine a new beginning

with too much to endure
before we sleep
before any new beginnings
could hope to begin

cars, like sanity, are driven
past huge old
mansion-like structures
architectural madness mixed with mirth and metaphor

housed in our brains – red brick matter
ancient, moss-covered, gothic sense
made out of
mortar and madness

fifteen cottages with fancy porticos
adorning massive columns
pseudo-Victorian mansions
ivy-covered with tunnels connecting each ward

tunnels of not enough love
clichés for the kooky
to adorn our minds
asking ourselves if this is at all a good route to follow

this decaying adornment, this labyrinth
to run through but never getting to the exit without bumping
into the same dead end a few hundred times
without realizing you have to fly right out of there

like Icarus – the father motif – Daedalus egging his son on
we all know how that turned out
wax-winged boy and doting dad
had some great ideas

too bad it all turned to well, shit

fifteen identical buildings sinking into crap-filled madness
was I the lucky one getting number 13?
all grouped together beside the lake
surrounded by fields of filth

crap left behind by winged creatures tethered
caught – in an orbital maze
finding the good sense God gave geese
to fly the fuck right out of there

out of Cottage 13…

Cottage 13

Cottage 13

*What do you think you are, for Chrissake, crazy or somethin'?
Well you're not! You're not! You're no crazier than the average
asshole out walkin' around on the streets and that's it.*
— *Ken Kesey, One Flew Over the Cuckoo's Nest*

take my word for it
you never wanna spend six months
in a place called Cottage 13
that is — not if you can help it

of course, nobody in there *could* help it…
never wanting to admit
we were actually in
a mental hospital

who would?
nurses pretending
we were all gathered together
in a "therapy unit"

the rest of the patients who needed drugs
were kept under lock and key
somewhere else on the grounds
people don't like to call themselves nuts

but nuts *sounds* way better than insane

Cottage 13 a moth-eaten mansion facing the lake
like something right out of *The Great Gatsby*
not *The Great Gatsby* of the early chapters
where Daisy and Jay think they might have a second chance

The Great Gatsby after the swimming pool scene
once the place has gone to pot
and the head of the house
has bled into the pool

but at first glance
even with its ominous tone
slightly decaying air
it really was beautiful

try it – squint a little
imagine all your memories
far more positive
than they really were

Cottage 13
and the surrounding grounds were
well – quite beautiful
from a warped romantic perspective

despite having
to avoid piles
of crazed goose shite
everywhere you walked

beautiful grounds crying in crap
just like my memories
but there's a silver lining, right?
tell me there's a silver lining

I'm still looking for it
maybe I'll find it here
in my shit-covered
memories

once in a while a madman would come wandering
this crazy bastard, screaming he was Jesus Christ,
would spot me and shout,
"And there she goes — it's Mary Magdalene,"

always smiling seemed pretty harmless
I'd see him out there, me in my sunglasses,
even in the rain with my rubber boots
even in the sunshine

there we'd be: Mary Magdalene and Jesus Christ
trying to find our way
lurching across black
fields of madness

there were twenty-seven of us
forced to live together in
that asylum by the sea
some of us with serious emotional problems

which is why we ended up there in the first place
I guess it's kind of mean of me to call us all loco
even when I include myself
but loco is always the first

word that comes to mind
when I think of that time
in Cottage 13

group therapy every goddamn day
sitting on ugly green couches
nurses in our group
so very pleased

when someone broke down
proof of a breakthrough
ready to deal with their pain

never felt comfortable
talking about Rick
and everything that happened
so I kept my mouth shut

and sat silently on the fringe
        like some kind of ghoul

Patsy Cline Crazy

it wasn't like the people there weren't trying to help
went out of their way to make us feel anything *but* crazy
some good people but generally speaking, everyone

staff and patients alike, were all a bit off
strong kind of crazy – Patsy Cline crazy
song of the love loons
like good coffee

like the dark-haired men
I learned to crave
strong and crazy
brawn and hazy

filtered though as the music and the booze played on

you could say that it was all a little off kilter
like a Gothic thriller, a film or a book
with half-crazed characters wandering through the
pages and the scenes and the goose poo

only difference was
we couldn't just switch
off the insanity like old movies
on a late-night TV set

set on the night table – then switch off the light
just go to sleep
or wander out of the movie theatre
taking all those images imbedded in your brain

back into a normal life
learned one normal thing there
and so many other places
learned there's

no such thing – no normal

something I should have seen coming
driving in that little Falcon
with my lovelorn first lover
headlong into life

"Normal" as fiction – like films or stories –
only exists on the page
something everyone tries to capture
call it their own kinda normal

some of us get there
more slowly than others
detoured by Cottage 13

Moths, Champagne & Stars

*In his blue gardens men and girls came and went like moths
among the whisperings and the champagne and the stars.*
— F. Scott Fitzgerald, The Great Gatsby

instantly depressed – already knowing
what it felt like to be depressed
being introduced to an even deeper level of
sadness and despair

walking into the main hall
seeing all the patients sitting around
smoking cigarettes and doing absolutely nothing
I knew I had problems but this was ridiculous

having serious doubts – wondering at the sanity of
the shrink I had met
(under dubious circumstances: in a bar, of course)
who had recommended that I go to this place for therapy
saying it would undo years of emotional damage

but bars had always made things seem
clear and beautiful to me
there, in the dim lighting and seductive grime
I could take the advice of a qualified stranger

walk right into a brand-new solution
this was no brand-new solution
enter, a doctor by the name of Henderson
walked out of his office, said something funny making me laugh

Dr. Henderson was English
blessed with that droll national wit
morbid, cynical and absurd: my kind of shrink
one of the good guys in a place filled with insanity

later, he told me a story about the village where he came from
discussing how eccentric we
sometimes could be
he segued into a story

about an old man he had known when he was a kid
the old fellow – around eighty, had been in the army
the village had rough stone walls like fences
about six feet high in front of every house

instead of walking down the street, the old man would walk
along the walls
people would look out the window
there he would be, just strolling along

with his head twelve feet in the air
if he saw you, he gave you the old army salute
very strange but no one thought anything of it
just accepted him

finally, irrevocably
irreversibly, a nurse
took me up to my room
horrified to find it was just a cubicle

with a smelly guy on the other side of the
flimsy green curtain separating us
flimsy green curtains the colour of shit
that's how I remember it

I'll write a song some day
for the ghost of Patsy Cline to sing
as a medley with "Crazy"
called "The Goose Shit Blues"

I go out walking
after midnight
out in the goose shit
singing I love you

ugly green curtains
separating me
from the loons
I wasn't crazy – *they* were

no privacy
everyone sleeping
in the same dorm
the size of a gymnasium

felt like something right out of
One Flew Over the Cuckoo's Nest
bothered the hell out of me
but what could I do?

shown my lovely new room
with the shit-green curtains
left my stuff and went back downstairs to meet
my new dysfunctional family

Nancy

To be ill adjusted to a deranged world is not a breakdown.
— Jeanette Winterson

walked through the common room
Nancy slid up and introduced herself
she was beautiful – seemed normal to me
what did I know? – normal to me who doesn't believe in
normal

Nancy asked if I liked to play Scrabble
she played all the time
thought she was going to beat me and beat me bad
little did she know that Scrabble was my sane game

making webs of words from scrambled blocks
everything I had taught myself

about love and life in my room –

family boys and booze from books

Scrabble was my refuge…

why she was there – Nancy – my God!
what I found out later could really curl your toes
wouldn't call her a raging nymphomaniac
but close – with plenty to rage about

everyone lounging around in ratty bathrobes
Nancy took it as her cue to
come slithering down the stairs
in a see-through negligee

some of the men thought it funny
especially the resident sex freaks
didn't understand it was the only way Nancy
thought she could get attention

had no self-esteem whatsoever

Nancy's father a big shot, a rich guy
never around — thought she was still
going through a difficult phase
even though she tried to kill herself three times

pretty much ignored her
began to realize
even though we were
very different from each other

seeing Nancy wander, barely clothed
through those haunting rooms —
among those shit-shod fields
along hallways down the stairs into common rooms

alluring, albeit inappropriate attire

we were all ghosts in see-through skin
all trying to hide; all different, all the same
all looking for the attention we needed
to feel better — sometimes the attention

just made us feel worse
more transparent as we
tumbled into sight

we, the
ghosts of the people
we were, the people
we wanted to be

barely clothed

Nancy, barely formed us…

Cottage Drama

Each morning
Cottage 13
woke us
all up

ungodly hour
6 a.m.
all stumbling
down to

breakfast – slumped
grim – one
bad coffee after another
smoked millions

of cigarettes
had quit
smoking the
year before

but began
to rethink
that decision – in
Cottage 13…

9 a.m. – filled with
caffeine and nicotine
all herded together
into the main room

community meeting
where I quickly discovered
things could get even hairier
than expected

a very scary biker dude
starts screaming
at another patient
nicknamed "the fart"

he slept in the cubicle next to me
frequent evidence
of his flatulence
was mind-numbing to say the least
        the less said the better

there he was, the little fart
and the big scary biker yelling
accusing Fart Face
of using his shampoo

began pushing each other around
almost turned into
an all-out brawl
(please, no blood!)

all the staff just looked on
as completely impassive
as they
possibly could

they had seen it all
found it somewhat squalid
like Salinger's "For Esmé –
with Love and Squalor"

raise high the roof – look in
you'll see the loons
fly around in cages
as pigeon shit staff puts up with it

expressionless fakes
couldn't care less
about the
patients

nurses pretended sincerity
fussed over patients
when the doctors were around
but as soon as we were alone – the fuss was over

each patient had two main nurses
meeting with us at least once a day
mostly the doctors were invisible
when caught in the halls

they seemed to be slinking
along corridors
hoping against hope
they wouldn't

run into – collide
with one of the loons
who made their bread and butter
impossibly possible

doctors ladders
snakes and scrabble
mostly men
mostly women

nurses on the lower rung
doctors, in the highest niches
hospital hierarchy

nurses below
patients on the bottom
some psychologists too
selected for you

but mostly we
were assigned to a single nurse
with the dubious title of "Prime Nurse."
she was on call, all the time

so you could have someone
to whom you could complain
whenever the urge struck

all worked as a team to figure
out what our problems were
how they could help us
deal with them

hospital offerings – like bird droppings
all kinds of brainless programs
drama, art therapy, belt-making, garden therapy
I chose sleep

being told
this was
a sure sign
of depression   (oh! was I depressed?)

wanting to say
there was no way
I'd be missing
my naps

having napped every day
long before I arrived
at this
godforsaken place

the one thing I'd come
to enjoy most in life
Scrabble in my sleep – reading into dreams
with no one to compete with the words and me

awake to take part in "Psychodrama"
the word alone says it all – dramatic
and definitely
for psychos

first day in their whacked-out little program
we stood in a tiny circle
were told to put one hand
on the shoulder of the person

with whom
we felt
the least unscathed

psy
cho
dra
ma

felt a tad uneasy
with sixteen different
sweaty paws weighing down
both my shoulders

it was
drama alright
and it
was psycho

little clinical theatre group
did wonders for my self-esteem
really made me feel like part of the 'family'
the dysfunctional one I wanted to escape from

but needed
to try
to put
up with

after humiliating scenes
everyone clamping
their mad, clammy palms on my shoulders
we had to pick a partner

a partner with whom we
would like
to be stranded
on a desert island

choosing someone
suitably somber
I spoke
of my sister — my calm in a storm

speaking fondly
I could overhear the doctor
telling his partner
he would like to be stranded with

Marilyn Monroe — even though she's dead, for chrissakes
just what a girl needs to hear
making it exceedingly obvious why she preferred to sing of
diamonds — not men — for friendship…

after *that* little drama we were given plastic bats
told to pretend to visit our dark side
beat the cushions which were spread out
all over the room

time for a mad nap

Me and Sylvia

Is there no way out of the mind?
  — Sylvia Plath

me and Sylvia
needing a bell jar
to hide in
to sleep...

if I was going to beat the daylights
out of something, it sure as hell
wasn't going to be a cushion
            I *loved* cushions

my head resting on one, on a bed, with me
asleep

as they say
as my parents
seemed to
silently say

to me

out of
sight
out of mind

Wishing, Praying

But I'm just a soul whose intentions are good.
Oh Lord, please don't let me be misunderstood.
— The Animals

God, how I wished
to be anywhere
but Cottage 13

with its decaying, Gatsby-esque ambience
I began to realize this was what Gatsby
was all about in the first place – not glamour – but decay

glamour
                        in

                                        decay

for which I needed a dentist, not a shrink
and surprise! I got one!
my own personal dental dreamboat would find me

in Cottage 13
but in the meantime
my worst fears were coming true

I thought
even the staff
couldn't see me for what I was

lonely and shy
no self-esteem.
emotional neglect had taken its toll

childhood had taught me
to withdraw
and withdraw I did – into Cottage 13

afraid of people
often difficult for me
to feel that I fit in

always looking
for secret spaces
stranger places

men and nurses
hungry ears
for hungry eyes

when I wasn't sleeping
my head was in a book
no way to enhance my social standing at the Cottage

but "Why," I thought
"Do I have to make friends?"
I was there to get help from the pros
       "was I not?"

I wasn't supposed to be
competing in a goddamn popularity contest.
Did they not understand what an introvert was?

I was angry with everyone
with the goofy therapist
who had told me that if I attended this therapy

it would help undo
so much bloody damage
sounded good at the time

in a nutshell, I was a guest
in a nuthouse
and I didn't understand

why I was
there
in the first freaking place

True Stories, False Teeth

1. groceries

just go grocery shopping
avoid the crowds
weekday
midday

a little old lady
approaches me
very sweet-looking
just stops

gently puts
her hand
on the edge of
my shopping cart

smiles and says
"I'm so sorry
about your skin condition, dear.
It looks very serious."

my lucky day
a retired dermatologist
takes pity on me
as if – some friendly intruder could tell me

the secret of life

"It's not acne,"
I protested
"It's eczema – I get it when I'm really
stressed out" – like now

get your poor old
hands off my grocery cart
but I said nothing…

"What a pity, my girl,
a young and beautiful
thing like you
with your whole life ahead of you."

wanting to
tell her to stuff
her pity in a plastic bag
with her tarts and oranges and Metamucil

knot the bag
and suffocate
all that unsolicited
goodwill

but no – true to form
I told her the whole, sordid tale
grocery carts stunned between us
glistening well-lit produce listening on

before I got to the really bad parts
I stopped – she had become so dejected looking
strained but sympathetic sadness in her eyes
finally she took her hand from my cart

stumbled away, horrified – finally…

I thought to myself
she's the crazy one – not me
she walks up to a stranger
in a grocery store

says something personal to them…
what did she expect?
I needed professionals
not sweet little old ladies

who thought it
perfectly normal
to share their concern
about my weeping complexion

I just wanted a box of Cheerios
and a quiet stroll through the cool aisles
and the calming produce
and the packaged claims to healthy living

not the sweetness
of ripened palms
on metal bars on carts
with wheels I'd rather fly away on

than listen
to your helpless love
your false smile

when the stories I have to tell
just crack that grocery grin
like the one

about the *dentist*…

2. teeth

You lose your laugh and you lose your footing.
– Ken Kesey

travelled his own
long and twisted path
had done extremely well
in his first couple of years in Dental School

by third year – cooking LSD
in his own private lab
for friends
a few lucky profs

managed to graduate
didn't realize the party was over
went back to where he was born
and started his practice

unfortunately, most of the town
had exceptionally good teeth
there he sat – filling his empty dental chair
experimenting with various pharmaceuticals

laughing his practice away
liked to combine drugs
but finally settled on
his professions' oldest joke

nitrous oxide, laughing gas

but this happy dentist had it in reverse —
lost his footing then found his laughs
too much laughter when the receptionist
found him unconscious one Monday morning

still hooked up to the gas
mask covering his face
lying in his chair looking
blue and very undignified

had been indulging in his own private joke
since the Friday before
lucky for him the gas ran out
he got the last laugh

The American Dental Association
found it no laughing matter
in his substance abuse
got three months in Cottage 13

developed a flattering crush on me
until my nurse, Dianna, burst my bubble.
"You think you're pretty cute, don't you?"

"No!" I exclaimed.
"Well, the staff have noticed
you seem to spend an

inordinate amount of time with the *Dentist*

one of the nurses noticed
the two of you sitting
on the couch together
last night, looking fairly cozy."

"We were watching TV
where else would we sit?
I can't help it if he likes me."
"We have very strict rules here

one of them being
there is no fraternizing between patients."

"And fraternizing is what, exactly?"

>patients considered to be spending
>too much time with one another
>and not a lot of time with everyone
>else

falling in love
in the nuthouse
is never
a good idea

"Well, I can't help if he likes me" I repeated –
sputtering, half embarrassed
but loving my laugh-lined – my gas guzzling
my own private *Dentist*

and then my own private nurse
said something
I shall never forget:
"Of course he likes you. *HE'S SICK!*"

I realized then
I was being watched
even when I thought I
was safe from prying eyes

I needed to be more cunning – more devious
plans would have to be made
like me – *True Stories, False Teeth*

I believed the ones that creased

my own private laugh lines –

        S
        sCrabbled
        R
        scAred
        B
        B
        bLed
        E . . .

Dianna

It takes two to speak the truth — one to speak and another to hear.
— Henry David Thoreau

Nurse Dianna — my angelic nurse
met at the most ungodly hours
little impromptu midnight therapy sessions

sound asleep in my little cubicle
Dianna would shake me awake
make me get up for a therapeutic chat

beautiful and bizarre
but hey, the nurses talked to you on
their schedules, even if the timing was completely unorthodox

I knew the last thing I needed after midnight
was a little talk about familial relationships
but there was something about her

even half-asleep, she made me want to talk
in her amazing English accent
she loved to talk to me, too

with books and an appreciation of humour in common
she could make me laugh
in a way, I had forgotten how — to laugh

a free-floating, uninhibited laughter
in the far reaches of Cottage 13
away from other voices

beginning by exchanging pleasantries
quickly getting down to business
my complaints about the other patients

how they didn't understand me
thought *I* was peculiar
because I liked to work out and didn't smoke

the women were all condescending
the men were assholes — dickheads to be precise —
treated me like an outsider

called me an aloof bitch — with problems
aloof, I was not — shy and introverted
are crosses I bear

like the crucifix we Catholic children
are asked to pray through into adulthood
I prayed in solitude

for a way through
this shit-storm
and got called a stuck-up bitch

guessing I must have made
the wrong impression
on condescending inmates and dickheads

wishing people had recognized
that difference about me
and not mistaken shyness and introversion

for
self-willed
isolation

we were all in the same sinking boat
throwing each other overboard
when we could have been sharing life rafts

remembering my first session with Dianna
the way I held back certain information
I had only one hour with her

didn't feel comfortable at first
but her warm and friendly manner
eventually wore down my resistance

I slowly began to trust her
I began to feel
I could tell her anything

anything at all
without fear of being judged
only when she began to delve

a little too deeply
I would veer off
discuss only the present – not the past

I beat against the past

I couldn't believe the
things that had happened to me
when I was younger

had so much to do with
the fact that I was such a mess now
but Dianna convinced me

I began to look
forward to our strange little chats
the other nurses were just nurses

maybe one or two of them had
some psychological training but that was it
I know because I asked them

knowing I needed someone
to talk to, who would listen to me
really hear me and feel how I felt

but why I would want
to put another person through
stories of all that had happened

finally realizing I was the other person
who didn't want go through it all again
and the nurses – they were getting paid

and that
I could understand
a pretty, good job – nursing at Cottage 13...
if you think about it

just show up and talk to inmates
who weren't going to die
on you or anything – hopefully

there was no blood or vomit
or other unmentionable
secretions to deal with just – stories

well, maybe the odd slasher in the
communal bathroom – fresh blood pooling
upon ancient tiles

but there were janitors to clean that stuff up

a blessing I had Dianna
who seemed to soothe

my shattered soul
I had to tell someone the whole story
so I could understand it myself

I would sit and talk with Dianna
for as long as I could stretch it
she was trying to protect me from situations

that seemed
inevitably
to arise

like Marshall, Judith, all the distant friends
       I'd made in Cottage 13
Marshall — the tooth decay doctor finding me
       in a rotting mansion
a glamour gone wrong narrative — mine

catching me — caught
between stories
I didn't see coming

torn — between
a funny nurse
and a laughing dentist

Dr. Walker

only a few weeks in Cottage 13
for Nurse Dianna
to call in the big guns

Dr. Walker – a large man
with a passion for, of all things –
bush planes –

office decorated with
miniature aircraft and logos
from all over North America

mixed with
a smattering
of baseball hats

I had to lay out my squalid history – again
all the while frantically making excuses
for all the bad choices – all the wrong turns

leading me to his bush-plane sanctuary
his head down, scribbling furiously
immortalizing my sad story in frowns
slight grins and hasty notes

every once in a while
raising his head
his face shone concern at me
from beneath bushy eyebrows

I liked him at once – maybe a little too quickly
that was one of the reasons I was there

I tended to be
        impulsive
especially when it came to
        trusting men
this horrible fear of being
        abandoned

I had always had it, ever since childhood

with elderly parents
appearing to be
on the verge
        of passing away

that was the first institution
I ever lived in — the whacked out 'retirement home'
where I was raised by my brothers

and unintentionally abandoned
by aging parents who seemed more like
grandparents at the time
        kindly, negligent, grandparents

a lack of trust creeping into my veins
causing me always
to be on high alert

in struts Dr. Walker — into my life at Cottage 13
could this bush plane — loving doctor
be the one to whom I could tell my innermost secrets?

the secrets I hid from everyone?
seeming so nurturing
seeming so normal

with his homespun collections
surrounding him
in his cozy little office hangar

"Tests show a few problems, Jet."

Post-Traumatic Stress Disorder – *not so bad*
Acquired Brain Injury – *not so bad*
Substance Abuse – *not so good!*

"Are these sessions confidential?" I ventured
"Yes, of course they are," he assured me.
and I replied,

"Because I don't want
them getting hold of this
information.

They could really crucify me with it."

He said, "Please don't worry,
you can trust me. Everything
you tell me is completely confidential

"I am not required to share it with
the staff – anyway, that's enough for today.
We'll begin discussing a treatment plan
during our next session."

As I rose to leave, in my nervousness
I knocked his bush plane cap
from its peg – it was stencilled with the words
"Lake Woebegone"

I walked back down
those grim green corridors and thought
"This might work out."

scurrying back to my "room," I passed Nancy
the sadly seductive lingerie lady
clad in yet another flimsy, see-through blouse

playing Scrabble with
a frightful guy named Lenny. (Don't name your son
Lenny – it sounds like a name a serial killer would have.)

I had given up Scrabble
taken up smoking again
I went outside to "the pit"

all the eating disorder people
were pressed together there – I don't know why
but they all stood in a cloud of smoke

"Spread out!" I thought. "Take in the fresh air
mix it up a bit, let the tobacco and God's blue
sky enter your lungs together

contemplate the fucking universe
stop puffing in packs, you insane
chain-smoking lunatics!"

instead I sat off by myself
in a state of high anxiety; self-righteous,
smoking, loner-angel-anointed bitch that I was

this was what usually happened
when I
pulled off the top

of the cauldron
that was my past
my pain
       my ecstasy
              my secrets
                     bubbling over

Two Bitches – One Cottage

1. Judith

from the twenty-seven patients
in our fragile little world
I really only got to know

a handful of the women
and made a few friends
one of them was named Judith

travelled with her
to Venezuela
soon after we were sprung

she had arrived late one evening
near the end of my stay
by the following morning

she had the whole place in an uproar
screaming at the nurses
accusing the doctors of not taking an interest in her

causing utter chaos
we were instant friends
I admired her spunk

later found out
her hot Latin temper
hid a broken heart

2. *Caroline*

and then there was Caroline – the bomb – hilarious
blessed with beauty and wit
called me "Beauregard" one day
       – out of the blue, just as a joke

came from a small town in Ohio
where her addiction to Demerol
had spun out of control

you could say it was her drug of choice
although she loved, *loved* to drink
and smoke pot too

one day Caroline told me
why she was addicted to this particular drug
she explained in loving detail

"Demerol will help you do anything you want
if you're tired, it will help you relax and sleep
if you've got stuff to get done, it will make you fly"

I filed that information in my "to do" list
I knew a few doctors and nurses on the outside
they, too, had become addicted to Demerol

Caroline felt she hadn't really reaped the full benefits
of her Demerol addiction because she hadn't had
the chance to stick it in her arm

she wanted to mainline it directly to her brain
I knew what she meant – if I'd had my druthers
I would have been a junkie in grade two

Caroline's sister was a nurse
through her, Caroline
learned how to phone in prescriptions under phony names

she would pick a different identity
a different disguise every time
she picked up her order

since there were only three drugstores
in the little town nearby
her options were limited

it was only a matter of time
before her luck ran out – one day
the pharmacist

refused to believe the fedora
the trench coat
and the long, grey hair, framing

that young, gorgeous face before him
belonged to 64-year-old
Ernie McCarthy

for Caroline – it became – it was
Cottage 13
or jail

Detroit City

Tennis Tale – Love Fifteen

1. murder city/murder ball

Windsor, Ontario, my Canadian city
across the river from Detroit, Michigan
Murder Capital, U.S.A.

driving over the Ambassador Bridge
even at five or six it always
felt like a dangerous place

the bridge that took you further
west of the danger
where relatives lived

we had seen the '67 riots
watched Detroit burn
our parents took us to Steinberg's

the top of the parking garage
the Motor City melting
I was too young, too young

to see such hate
such fearful violence
how do you fathom seeing a whole city in flames?

not to mention people thrown off
the Belle Isle Bridge
into the dirty river over drug wars

"the pink chemical nights"
those factory sunsets seen
from our sick house below

this was my childhood sunset foreshadowing
            drugs and death
unsung picnics by the water – sex and disappointment
would follow me back across those bridges

over a river where
factories dumped their sludge
Zug Island Rouge River Detroit River

we couldn't swim when I was a kid
a river of rot floating downstream
but we could picnic by the water

my elderly dad
sitting on our front porch chair
with his respirator and walking stick

while all the other fathers on the block
ran up and down the street with their kids
throwing footballs around

four older brothers
one in Vietnam
the rest at home – persecuting me

once, brother Liam
threw a glass bottle at my head
missed because he's such a twit

hit my other brother, Jack
splitting his little head open
Ouuuuuuuughhhh…

I can still see the blood
gushing from his head
into the tub and hear my mother's screams

as usual, Liam got away with it
because, after all, the bottle was
meant for me

hitting Jack was an accident.

since I was the baby
you would think my parents
would have spoiled me rotten

well, you're right, and wrong
they did whatever they could
for me – and more

saving me – for themselves
from themselves

2. *my first racquet*

Tennis is the loneliest sport.
— Andre Agassi

when I was seven years old
my brother brought home
my first tennis racquet
he'd bought it in Saigon

while he was on leave
grabbed that racquet and never looked back
when spring sprung
that year, every single, bright, shiny day

would find me on skinny legs
crossing the street to the high school
where I could be found relentlessly
banging tennis balls against the wall by the hour

obsessive/compulsive — perhaps

sweating and panting
making myself hit the ball
one hundred times in a row
with one bounce

before I allowed myself to go home

pretty soon I was competing
in tennis tournaments
and not doing badly
by the time I was ten

everyone thought I was
the next tennis sensation
I would hang around the courts
when the high school kids were

receiving their lessons
coach eventually noticed me
and saw me play
I guess he liked what he saw

because he started including me
in the tennis lessons – had me demonstrate
the different strokes, to the
big, high school kids

Lou Veres, my tennis coach,
called me Tiger
if only he had known
how apt that nickname would turn out to be

my freckled mug was frequently in the paper
and I developed quite a
reputation as "the one to watch"
soon, I was travelling all over the country
        playing junior tennis tournaments

won enough matches to obtain a ranking
and that's heady stuff, especially for a kid
        the only disappointment

was being subjected on a daily basis to the
hefty rear-view of our chaperone, Mrs. Porter
seventy, wore bright red lipstick and mini-tennis dresses
she drove the junior players
      to all our tournaments

it was embarrassing to be seen with her because
she insisted on wearing those obscene tennis whites
wherever we went — she never changed those clothes

the car trips were torture because she had
an aggravating habit of surging forward
then decelerating

all the way, down the highway

we would be carsick by the time we reached the tournament
because of the horrid rocking motion
we had endured the entire journey

between the vista presented by her backside
and the roller coaster road trips
this girl was nearly driven crazy

it wasn't long before the pressure of playing top-level tennis
began to wear on me — I had no other life
and I was only seventeen

tennis was great
but I looked around
saw that my friends
from school

had begun to dabble in sex, drugs and rock'n'roll
I began to wonder if I wasn't missing something
of course, in hindsight, I wasn't missing anything

I should have followed my own path but I didn't

what a mistake!

the strain of having
to retain my tennis ranking
was wearing me down

one weekend I would play
some superstar from California
and manage to beat her

but would have to face her
at the next tournament
one match was enough

tennis players began to unnerve me
I would arrive at the tennis club in fairly good spirits
ready to play

thinking what a great game
tennis was
I would spot my opponent

in 200 dollar tennis shoes
carrying three racquets – what a schmuck!
my opponent would stomp

onto the court, glower at me
the game would begin
each time I won a point

she would give me the look from hell
and her parents would gesticulate angrily
shout encouragement at her

from behind the fence
it was maddening
my spirits would sink

I'd stare down at my old, beat-up, black running shoes
that I had covered with graffiti
and wish I could be anywhere else

I would dream I was playing centre court at Wimbledon
dressed in black and the girl on the other side of the net
was civilized and not nuts like most of my opponents

it ceased being a game – would quickly turn into a bloodbath
I started to lose important tennis tournaments
and my ranking began to slip

I began to dread facing crazed opponents
with their bulging eyes and murderous faces
turning bright red in their half-crazed efforts to win

they had to win – for them there was no other option
they would fight
to the brutal end

after hours and hours
running around in the hot sun
I realized that I would much rather be

sitting on the sidelines
with an ice-cold Coke
and a cigarette

I would let them win
my intense need to prove myself the best
was quickly dissolving

I seemed to lack that inner drive, that killer instinct
how I would wish one day that I had stuck with tennis
so clean, so wholesome, so *sane*

3. love one lost

*I hate to advocate drugs, alcohol, violence, or insanity to anyone,
but they've always worked for me.*
    — *Hunter S. Thompson*

I once told Dianna
my funny, protective nurse
about the first time I took LSD

playing in a major tennis tournament
my ranking depended on its outcome
vitally important I win this tournament

to secure my spot in the Top 10
the night before, my high school friend Mia and I
had driven to the National Tennis Centre
        in my Volkswagen Bug

four hours to get there and when we did
we stopped just long enough to drop our bags off
I was being billeted at a snooty private school

had to sneak Mia into my room
we changed into skin-tight black jeans
headed downtown to score some dope

had heard about an area in the city
where we could find what we were looking for
Mia had already tried it with Neal, her pusher man

she was anxious that I try it, too

I approached the first vaguely drugged-up looking guy
I saw and asked, "Do you have any acid?"
"Sure man. I've got Windowpane and Purple-Microdot.

"Which one do you want?"
"The purple one. I like that colour."
little did I know I had chosen the most potent variety

I followed him down an alley and made the deal
I gave him ten bucks for one hit
which I peeled from a piece of paper and swallowed

Mia didn't like the looks of him
she scooted across the street
to find another dealer
bought some mescaline and quickly downed it

we took the subway back to Upper Canada College
where the other tennis players were staying
hoping we wouldn't run into anyone
we scampered up the back stairs.

Mia was starting to look sick
before I knew it, she had thrown up
the mescaline with the cheeseburger she'd had for dinner
it was going to be a solo flight for me

I waited anxiously for the drug to take effect
didn't know what to expect
had only a vague understanding of what acid was
I kept waiting and waiting but nothing happened.

"It's been three hours since I took the acid," I said to Mia.
"How long is this stuff supposed to take to start working?"
"Don't worry," she replied. "It'll happen."
"I think I was ripped off, Mia.

Should we go downtown and get some more?"
She laughed and said, "NO! I'm going to bed.
just relax and go with the flow."
I lay down on my bed and cursed myself for being so gullible

all of a sudden, I started to feel
a strange tingling sensation in my throat
for some reason, I felt my skin was turning orange
this was strange
        – I got up to look in the mirror and I *was* orange!

"Oh, no!" I thought. "I'm all alone and I'm turning colours.
What have I signed on for?"
I would have thought if I was going to change colours
at least the colour would be purple

and all the tennis players would know
that I was playing with a handicap called microdot

I got up again and went to check
to see if the pupils of my eyes were
enlarged because someone had told me
that's how you got caught by the authorities

my pupils were so big that
my blue eyes had left the building
as I lay in bed, the walls began to undulate
looking as if the ceiling was melting down into the floor.

the radio was on but the music
        seemed to be coming from inside me

made my way out to the balcony
because I thought some fresh air might help
only to find that the trees were moving
and the leaves seemed to be slithering
        with psychedelic snakes

began to wonder if doing this acid
        had been such a great idea
I wanted it all to stop but Mia had told me
that it would last a good eight hours – at least

she also neglected to mention
that being able to fall asleep
would not be an option

I woke Mia and asked her what to do.
"Don't worry," she said. "Just go with the flow!"
"But my tennis tournament!" I cried.

"I gotta play in the morning!"
        she went back to sleep

as I gingerly made my way back to bed
which appeared to be five miles away
I began to get very freaked out
I tried to go to sleep but the hours sped by

in multicoloured hallucinations. Beautiful…

soon I could hear the other tennis players
walking down the corridor
on their way to breakfast
my first match was scheduled for 9 a.m.
        and I was a mess

I frantically tried to get myself together
showered with tennis whites on, I took the elevator down
when the doors opened, I faced a lobby full of
        shiny, healthy people.

I knew I had to eat if I was going to play my match

Mia had also neglected to tell me acid and food do not mix
as I reached for my orange juice, I was surprised to see
the animals on the cereal boxes prancing up and down
the long wooden breakfast table

could hear a cacophony of hundreds of different languages
coming from the rest of the tennis players
    – thought I was hearing things
then I remembered it was an international tournament
and there were people attending from all over the world

unable to eat I boarded the bus
        to be driven to the coliseum
my panic was so intense that I slunk to the back of the bus
took a seat by myself, hoping no one would notice me
        and realize how very stoned I was

we arrived and I carefully navigated the steps
        down from the bus
the shock of sunshine and heat almost knocked me over
slapped my face like molten lava

we shuffled into the clubhouse
and I was faced with the cold reality
of having to play my first match
against a top-seeded, west coast champ

I spied my opponent warming up
on the grass beside the tennis courts
stretching and bouncing
on her toes

infused with energy
in my drug-induced stupor, she appeared
to be well over six feet tall
'the attack of the giant tennis player!'

her name was Jennifer Sanderson
a tanned athletic Princess, which meant
I was up against top-flight
coaches and year-round play

while she was warming up with her personal coach
I was teetering on this side of sanity
I knew that I needed to cancel the match
but my ranking depended on the outcome of
        this fucking tournament

High on Tennis

dejectedly, I followed her and her racquets onto the court
with a sheepish look on my face
feeling like I was wearing a big, red
sign that said "Dirty Girl Does Drugs"

I was shaking – we started warming up
hitting the ball back and forth, all the while
checking each other out
and sussing out each other's weak points

I started to think that maybe I could pull this off

after all, I had beaten her before – or maybe that had been
her sister, Rose?
I was in no state to recognize anyone
five minutes into the match, I experienced
a strange phenomena

when I threw the ball into the air to serve
I saw five or six balls floating in the sun –
'tennis balls, in the sky, with diamonds'
couldn't tell which ball was real and which wasn't

found out later that it was called seeing *"trails"*
in a steady stream of neon yellow – my racquet had ten heads

the Loch Ness tennis monster
reeling out of control
at the end of my wrist
and I was losing control

    over the
            one thing
                    that had given me
                                    control

before I knew it
I was losing in a very big way
had not won one point in the first set
and the second set went just as badly

I lost 6-0, 6-0 – that's twelve games to nothing
Jennifer smiled maliciously at me
as she hurriedly made her way back
to the clubhouse to gleefully inform
        the tournament directors of her win

at this point I was beyond caring
just wanted to get out of the sun
and back to my room where I could have
a Coke and a cigarette

Mia was still sleeping
I felt like strangling her
because I had lost my ranking
I had had it.

I quit

        I lay my tennis racquet down

                      anxiously awaiting utopia

Bad & Sad
(more 'cottage' life – off the courts and into the rackets)

after all those years of 'fun'
tennis booze drugs boys becoming men
men becoming boys in my tanned arms my blue eyes
it wasn't easy to have my wings clipped

to be confined to the realization
of the gothic version of a novel I once loved:
> Cottage 13

fuck off Daisy fuck off Gatsby fuck off Scott

I'd experienced the aloofness of
bitches and their crazed parents
as a racquet tournament angel
with halos wrought from drug-induced auras

(not to mention the ample butt cleavage
of the insane tennis dominatrix, Mrs. Porter)
my membership in a gaggle of drug-loving teen angels
all with unique problems – we bonded like superglue

how had tennis even become part of the equation?
sometimes the right side of the tracks
meets the other side of the tracks
and it all goes terribly wrong

a cast of characters of
which I had yet to see the likes of anywhere
in lurid novels or over-the-top movies
yeah, former tennis angel in a nuthouse

me, honoured with the title of Mary Magdalene
to a delusional Christ figure
       – that Jesus-freak, wandering
through the goose crap, who called out to me
       from the muck
"Hey Mary, you look beautiful today"

in my rubber boots and lurking behind my Ray-Bans
plotting my escape from the frenzied fortress,
       I looked beautiful?
I left those muddy hospital grounds every chance I got
unfortunately, I had to depend on

the kindness of other nuts
to do so – sometimes I got lucky
there were some fine-feathered bitches in that place

and I
found me some
to fly the coop with
       whenever I got the chance

Anne *(one bitch one coat & me)*

struck up an acquaintance
with another patient
by the name of Anne – a bitch I bonded with

the nuthouse shopping expedition
was the highlight of our week
we both loved old thrift shops

I was always on the lookout
for really great stuff – I had five one hundred
percent pure Cashmere coats

she was on the lookout for a captive audience
in a speeding car
on the way to nowhere fast

bitching – ranting – re-telling trauma
just what I needed on a day off
from the nuthouse

we would take off on those afternoons
like bats out of hell
Anne always dressed in black and a

certifiable maniac behind the wheel
she would look over at me and say,
"Sometimes, I just want to drive this car
right into the lake."

I would smile weakly and reply,
"Don't worry. It'll get better,"
as if I really believed *that*

"Nothing has ever gone right for me," she'd continue
as she sped along," I may be seven years' sober
but I can't take this anymore –

I did all the stuff they tell you to do
and I'm more fucked up than when I drank –
at least then I didn't know I was depressed

I thought I was having a good time.
I mean, it's shit – never getting drunk again.
Never again! I don't even want to go there.

Everybody else has a bad day and can go out and
get wasted, me, I gotta sit around
and try not to kill myself.

What's the point?"

she whined on and on, whether I wanted to hear it or not
and in the back of my mind, I thought it might be better
if she just drove us *both* into the goddamn lake

but I made commiserating noises
she'd continue her sad-sack saga
Anne loved to talk about herself

batty as all get out, in her own private hell
driving like a bat right out of hell –
headed for the thrift shop

with dreams of a lake-deep respite
with me in the passenger seat
        dreaming of another Cashmere coat
Anne could not get enough of herself lamenting —

"At least I wasn't a pothead like my husband.
He had it around all the time
lying on the coffee table.

But he looked down at me cuz I drank.
I couldn't help it!
I would try to maintain

not drink more than anyone
else but I'd always end up
falling down somewhere

and totally humiliating
myself. It was like the Twilight Zone
one minute I would be sitting there

with a couple of friends, having a cocktail and the next,
I'd be coming to, in a strange bed,
in a strange place with a strange guy."

She talked on and on, relentlessly telling me
the ghastly things that always happened
when she blacked out

the first day we spent together, she
confided that her husband had
poured black paint all over her in the bathtub

and almost killed her
her pores couldn't breathe
fortunately, a friend heard her screaming,
    she was rushed to
the hospital and they managed to remove the paint
    to save her life

"I don't even remember why he dumped
that black paint all over me
and at this point I don't fuckin' care!"

As we sped along, I'd think,

Maybe she just needed a new paint job.

with a sidelong glance, she'd crank the volume
on the car radio, and blast raucous heavy metal

*No wonder she has problems; this music would
    drive anyone to drink.*

she would drive as fast as the music was loud
eventually, I would lean over and lower the volume
discovering, I could control her speed
by turning the music down

I was too stressed to complain
but I had to find a compromise
and it didn't seem to bother her

one night she took a sharp turn
around a corner at a speed of
fifty miles per hour and lost control

we ended up
facing the opposite
direction

on the grounds of the hospital
it was some surreal spin
right back to where we started

no lake
no thrift shop
no Cashmere coat

too embarrassed and traumatized to tell her
I had a thing about cars
my earliest memory of a car crash was when
       I was nine years old

I had been playing baseball on a summer evening
heard what I thought was a loud explosion
two cars had collided right behind me

I never forgot the sight of that head
with a bloody towel draped over it
sticking through the smashed windshield

of the vehicle nearest me
I know this experience resulted in my inability
to drive on highways later in life

my imagination was too vivid and cars and trucks
speeding by caused me to panic – except in the States
the roads were wider

there were more lanes – stress free
not like the 401
Americans were the most civilized drivers I knew

most people get defensive and angry with you when you ask
them to slow down, always demanding
you tell them what's wrong with their driving

I've always hated having to defend my position and not
admit my phobia or maybe I just knew the facts
the definition of someone who is

paranoid is someone who knows the facts (that's a joke)

I know now that I had an anxiety problem
but at the time, that was the least of my worries
I never did like things I couldn't control, especially

when control was in the hands of someone like Anne

I had already lost control
and had no intention of letting someone else lose *even more,*
for me

not for Anne
not for no one and not
for no second-hand Cashmere coat

Weekends

So we beat on, boats against the current,
borne back ceaselessly into past.
       – F. Scott Fitzgerald, The Great Gatsby

managed to convince the hospital
I really needed to be released on weekends
most of the patients had nowhere to go, no homes to visit
but I had an apartment in the city and I craved some solitude

allowed to leave at eleven each Friday morning
I would burst from group therapy
run to the closet, grab my coat and book
           as fast as humanly possible
race across the grounds with the speed of a cheetah

make a mad dash for the bus stop
I wondered what the bus driver thought of me
didn't want him to think I was one of the nuts
oh, no, not me. Beating against the rapid pace of my
           slow-motion madness

fuck off Scott with all your glamorous assholes –
I was born back ceaselessly into my apartment
where I could find a couple days' reprieve from
other people's pathologies I didn't sign up for

finally, I would get home,
amongst my beloved books and paintings
my lamps and my rugs

and my own bed – I was safe and sane
such sweet relief!
but my inner demons awaited me there,
too – and of course

I would have to return, *"back ceaselessly into the past"*

    when the weekend was over

Marijuana

first time I smoked marijuana
was not the mind-bending scenarios I had envisioned
for months, the anticipation of smoking pot –

blissfully floating away from everything and everyone
who had ever hurt me – was intense
I thought I would experience beautiful abandon

and dance righteously off
into the soft
October night

Mia came and picked me up
under the cover of darkness,
we made our way to Neal's house, downtown
off Erie Street, forbidden territory
        for a couple of Catholic girls –

on the wrong side of the tracks, so to speak

had a hard time finding his house
because the street was eerily lit
we couldn't see the house numbers

finally, we found the house and went around back
as had been previously instructed
Neal met us at the door with a knowing grin

led us down to the basement – his "den" was wild,
lit with black lighting – which made all the girls' bras
visible like headlights on our chests – surreal

Neal had psychedelic posters tacked up on every wall
and the smell of incense was exciting
Iggy Pop exploded through the room

making the scene all the more intoxicating
I wondered what his parents must have thought we were up to, down in the den
did they think he had a few friends over, playing Monopoly?

eating chips and drinking pop?

everyone clustered in groups of three or four
whispering to each other and probably wondering
what the hell Mia and I were doing there

I recognized a couple of people from school
and they greeted us with tuned-in eyes
this was a subversive little society we were infiltrating

and newcomers were regarded with suspicion
        our reputations had
proceeded us and we were generally thought
        to be "good girls" at school
we couldn't help but look out of place
        – got the feeling we were being scrutinized

funny, how my suspicions of constantly being eyeballed would
escalate dramatically in the years to come
but now I know it well – paranoia

Neal scurried off to his hidden stash
brought us back our nickel bag
the going rate was five bucks – not a bad deal

we handed over the money and sat on the floor,
>   trying to be as
unobtrusive as possible and pretending we knew
>   what the hell to do next
I mean, we now had the pot in our hot little hands
>   but what was the protocol?

did we not need something to smoke this stuff in?
a pipe, rolling papers, tea? How do we get stoned?
at this point in the evening

my excitement level had reached a crescendo
I had started to sweat
was just about ready to go ahead and eat the drugs

I didn't care what it tasted like – forget the paraphernalia and
just devour the stuff – Mia, always a little more composed
called someone over and asked them to roll us a joint

you know, just to get us started
>   nothing embarrassed her, ever
after the first hopeful puff, I waited
for the gates of heaven to swing open

"Did you get off?" asked Mia.
"Not yet," I whimpered.
Five minutes later, she asked again

"Did you get off?"
"NOT YET," I barked.
"Well," she exclaimed.

"Don't you feel anything at all?"
"What was wrong with me?" I thought.
Oh no! It wasn't working

I wasn't getting high.
I suggested we roll another one and maybe
    that might do the trick
we carefully gathered the pot in a little pile

Mia rolled us another one
we smoked that one up like two crazed weasels
inhaling each toke as if our very lives depended on it

I swallowed acrid smoke and held it deep
    in my lungs until
I thought I might pass out
the worst thing would be to start coughing
    and be unable to stop

thus exposing ourselves as the neophytes we were
after all, the whole idea was to fit in
it began to occur to me and my very skeptical mind
    that maybe

we weren't smoking real pot
    – was this really marijuana?
or was it just ground up grass
    – literally?
finally, we got Neal's attention and called him over

"Is this really pot?" we asked him.
"Is there something wrong with the weed?" we cried.
"Or was it just us?"

"Are we the only two people on the planet
    who can't get high?"

he anxiously explained that
the first time one smoked
marijuana, one might not get off.

"But there are two of us!" I exclaimed
we quietly unbent our legs and
ungracefully rose to our feet and left

the streetlights looked a bit odd
maybe something was happening
on our way home, walking and talking

which was when we decided to go back the next weekend —
if only for the atmosphere — right
two weeks later, I was a regular customer

buying my own private supply
and smoking joints frantically in the attic
or driving around in my electric-blue Bug

finding parking at a spot on the river, dreaming of love
while looking at the doomed ruins of Detroit City
remembering that parking garage

my elderly parents watching Detroit burn
now, marijuana, burning in my hand, at the end of my wrist
control leaving my body

like tennis balls flying through a purple haze

out
       of
               my
                       control

The Centres
– One Day's Journey Into…

1. Prelude

across the street
from an apartment
I once rented

lived a group
of sketchy, shifty guys
resembling bikers – for the most part

I always kept a wary eye out
they tended to occupy
their front porch

drinking all day
and into
the night

apparently keeping
an eye out on me
but in a good way

one of them
a different one
every time

would collect me
at night after
I had fallen out

of
my
taxi

he would politely
dutifully
cross the street

pick me up
carry me
up the stairs

to
my
apartment

one night, Eddie
from the group
across the way

called across
from their porch
asked me

to go
to a party
with him

the shindig
was
out of town

he assured me
it was a family
get-together

neglecting to tell me
he had four brothers
three sisters

all of them
raging drug addicts
living together

in a shack
in Hamilton —
oh, the squalor!

his *family* of coke addicts
pestered me
for hours

finally, I acquiesced
and told them —
"Sure, you can inject me"

I had
no fear
and less sense

I had never tried
to inject cocaine
into my bloodstream before

so some coked-up
dude – some brother, some sister –
injected it for me

immediately
                I
                              collapsed

when I came to
they were all standing
around me

not one of them
knew what to do
to help me

I crawled
on hands and knees
to the second-floor bathroom

started
throwing up
blood clots

"Oh, my God" – the anguish
this was serious shit
I was in

so far down
I did not see
any way out

was this
how I
was going

to live
my life?
for booze and drugs?

hanging out with
drug addicts
constantly jonesing

for my
next
high

when I
was on
my feet

I had noticed
a man earlier,
in the living room

who had not
had a drink nor
had he done any drugs

I asked him why
he was
abstaining

he told me
he had just
gotten out

of a
treatment centre
up north

"What's a treatment centre?"
I asked —
he answered —

"It's a hospital
that treats alcoholics
and drug addicts"

Oh, the squalor!

2. Get me out of here!

Some people never go crazy.
What truly horrible lives they must lead.
— Charles Bukowski

that one conversation
made me think
there might be a way
out of this mess

no more Cottage 13 for me!
addiction was my problem
not mental illness
maybe I had found a solution

I called the treatment centre
the following week
they gave me a date
just after Christmas

come in for a twenty-eight day program
I had no idea what I was doing
much less what lay ahead

The Treatment Centre's – that's what lay ahead…

3. North Bay Treatment Centre

didn't know I was an alcoholic
but I knew that everything was wrong
I would pass out, fall, split my head open

very attractive!

January, I took the midnight train to North Bay
shady characters, bitter security people
grumpy cab drivers

and one lost twenty-seven-year old

the only train to North Bay
wouldn't arrive till
four in the morning

a deserted little station with no lights and no one there
no people, no taxis, no nuthin'
it was Cottage 13 all over again with a different geography

standing in the parking lot
frightened and freezing
I noticed an empty taxi cab

I got in and locked the doors

an hour later
there were lights at the end of the road
the taxi took me to the centre

an old convent for retired nuns
looked like another of the
same old horrible gothic psychiatric hospital

I knocked on the big oak doors thinking
"Holy shit, is it the great fucking Gatsby again,
gone religious?!" Nobody answered

finally, a nurse opened the door, telling me I couldn't come in
it's freezing and it's five a.m. and she's saying,
"No, sorry; you'll have to come back at eight –
Go to the hostel until then."

three hours later
I waited on the steps in the cold
knocked again on the big oak doors

finally admitted into the centre
I was bleary-eyed and chilled
but, I was also in a beautiful room, overlooking a lake

no more goose shit – no more bitches
ranting and trying to drive me
into the depths of watery, terrified despair –
maybe this was a better place?

I thought to myself hopefully,
"I can do this
I can do this!"

then came a girl, knocking on my door –
"You have to come and
meet the community."

another
fucking
community

they had taken my suitcase
dumped it to look for razors
or aspirins or anything that could hurt me or get me high

I went with her
was introduced
to a room filled with 150 people

another version of Cottage 13

during the first two weeks
I kept hearing about
the hot seat

that it was very hard
to get past the hot seat
and stay in treatment

there was a nun
I worked with in treatment
who was gentle and kind

but the day I took the hot seat
she wasn't there – instead, I got the sadist Cam,
a "recovering" alcoholic with a goddamn clipboard

sitting in the middle of the room
on a little red stool with all the
other addicts around me

whatever any of them said, I couldn't defend myself
I had to take it all
they were trying to break me

that was the point of
the hot seat
but the clipboard wielding sadist got it all wrong

he somehow decided
I was looking for a guy with money
and he made it weigh heavily
as part of the whole hot seat treatment

I said, "No, that's not true," but he said
"Shut up,
you can't talk."

An older woman – in her sixties –
went the day before me and got the same sadist
with the fucking clipboard

he told her
stop playing with herself
her roommate had said she masturbated all night long

she left

there was another guy, from Quebec,
Cam accused of fucking sheep –
he left, too – the hot seat – it was unreal

after my first session on the hot seat
I got back to my room and someone had put
roses on my bed – I didn't know who

another whacked out, infuriating
Gatsby moment…a warm, romantic, gothic scene
filled with madness – I stayed.

I couldn't drink nor do drugs
but still couldn't see why these things were a problem
the substances weren't the problem

it was what happened in my mind
when I used them
that was the problem

booze and drugs – they were an escape
liquor and literature were my escape
not substance abuse nut substance recluse

that was me – or so I thought
at that first centre I met a guy
he was so funny – with woefully bad teeth

he lived in North Bay – we hung out together
when I got out of the centre
I popped a Valium

went straight to his place
he had been released the week before
we smoked pot but I refused to drink

years later I found out
he died of alcoholism
so tragic

I continued to relapse
after I left that first treatment centre
I could never get past more than
three or four months before something would happen

I would pick up a drink again
not utilizing the tools in place to protect me
I went into treatment again — every time

I drank, at home or at a party
I would lock the bathroom door
take all my clothes off and get into the tub

it was a period of suicidal blackouts
with cops breaking in to haul me out
maybe someone should have dumped paint on me,
like good ol' Anne

that might have snapped me out of it —
once a boyfriend took the bathroom door off
to get me out of my tropical womb

that treatment centre had managed
at the very least to convince me
I had a *problem*

Oh, the squalor!

4. Sanderson Treatment Centre – Toronto

an abandoned hospital
way out on Lakeshore
at the bottom
of Islington

seeing an actor named Joe
badly in love
we hung around the Cameron
an artsy bar on Queen Street

during the relationship
I decided I had to
go into treatment again
it was horrible

going out with these cool people
because I seemed to be
the only one who couldn't drink
or do any drugs

a menace to society after three or four drinks
I'd be in a blackout
I'd wake up in jail or a stranger's bed or
in the hospital

it was never just about drinking
it was more like inside my booze addled brain I was
thinking –
"I don't care,
I'm just going to die tonight."

but back to the centre – to get to the treatment centre for 8 a.m.
I needed to be up at 5 – I was an outpatient
they wanted me to stay in
but I refused

boils erupted on my ass
my first day at Sanderson
the place was
kind of nasty

I had a block: I couldn't understand
why I couldn't just smoke pot
I thought I could have a good time
not fall in the street or end up in hospital

the counsellors had a hard time making me realize
it didn't matter what substance
it was, but I had my mind
made up

thinking I was funnier
more attractive
when I drank or did drugs
romantic self-destruction

I was always felt so shy, self-conscious and embarrassed
I never felt right
felt apart from myself
when I drank

needing doubles of
everything
I could laugh along
and drink and socialize

everything felt okay, even though it was all
separate from who
I was — who I was
trying to be

but could never quite become —
before I could get anywhere, I'd black out
and there was no place to go
but down…

as they say —
down
down
down…

the thing is, alcoholics feel
they just don't fit in
with their families
with people in general

you don't want to talk
and never feel comfortable.
I met an actress at this particular treatment centre
I never would have stayed there

without her
a quirky funny beautiful talented actress
everyone loved her
as soon as we got out

that night, we got drunk together
a bar on Bloor Street
I don't know what happened
never found out

Blackout!

but it turned out, after that night
her friends didn't want her to see me
anymore – they thought I was bad news
I would visit her

before the big bust-up on Bloor
in her little apartment on Spadina
her bed covered with
big stacks of books

once we got out
of the centre
never saw her
again

didn't feel as if I fit in
at that treatment centre
years later when
I started to tell

my story to a new friend
he had known her
they were in a crazy play together
reciting poetry – different poems
at the same time

they drank together too
but he never remembered the drinking
being a problem
they were young

this coincidence took
me back and made
me want her in my
life again

but drinkers often
leave each other
when they see each other
or others see them

reflecting
their own addiction
in each other's
eyes

being at the Sanderson Treatment Centre
caused me to break up
with Joe
because he would call

at two in the morning
asking to meet him on Baldwin Street
an after-hours club
a booze can

I pleaded with him not to call
in the middle of the night
I would be forever
on the phone

he kept insisting
but I wouldn't meet him at the club
getting to the centre one morning
without any sleep

after talking to him
on the phone for two hours
when I got home late that afternoon
he was in my bed

in his underwear – I made him leave
we broke up; it was heartbreaking
a intense visceral pain
an aching sore my chest my stomach

I got out of the centre
lost my beautiful boyfriend
lost my wonderful actress friend
it was all about loss

I was looking for something and losing everything.

5. *Oshawa Treatment Centre*

two years after my stint at the Sanderson Centre
ended up in a centre in Oshawa
a house full of women
six to a room

all slept in little beds: a factory; a platoon!
no more gothic fucking mansion/convents
for me – good riddance, Gatsby!
      – I love you, but fuck off Scott!

the woman next to me would hiss,
Turn off the fuckin'light!
because I would read at night
      – the only way I could fall asleep

she told everyone
she used to go to
Charlie Manson's ranch
and ride his horses

"How could that be?" I wondered.

I felt uncomfortable and alone
and I didn't want to be there
I would stay up
most of the night

slept on whatever couch I could find
for a few hours – exhausted and miserable
felt so apart from everyone else
I decided not to stay

the women who ran the house meant well
but it was not helping me
whatsoever
I called a cab one night and left

I toughed it out for two weeks
and I remember
as I left that place

the Manson woman screamed at me,

You fucking bitch, what happened to you?
You're beautiful and
you threw it all away!
Why?
I don't understand!

no one understands
it's an allergy of the body
a mental obsession
of the mind

a disease.

like me
like all my fine feathered friends
feeling nervous and worried

and as soon
as we have a
drink, suddenly

it's like someone
hits us over the head
with a great big log

and we collapse with relief

6. Ohio – Jackson Hill Treatment Center

a year after Oshawa I got lucky
a very good rehab facility in Ohio
geared for medical people

doctors, nurses
pharmacists
& me

I managed to get in as I
had a friend, a doctor
who got me in: I stayed six months

I met yet another *friend*
which wasn't good because
they didn't want us to hang out

together

they said we'd be thinking too much
about each other and not about our own
recoveries – now I understood

he was a surgeon – a lovely, kindhearted guy
we took off one weekend not supposed
to leave the center

but I needed to pick up some Christmas presents
he took me to Columbus
slept on his friend's couch and went back Monday

that afternoon the alarms went off
and someone said through the speakers
everyone to the main hall

five hundred people were in that center
all medical people with addictions
& me
at one meeting the woman who ran the program

asked if anyone could tell her
if I had gone away
with the surgeon

for a weekend in Columbus?
it was intense because if they caught him
he would lose his license – he needed

three months of treatment
it was important that no one tell on us
a fellow housemate squealed on us privately

but said nothing
that day in the meeting room
we were allowed to stay

her tattling didn't work because
no one else would confirm what she said
she wasn't a reliable a source

I stayed there for six months
stayed clean and sober for six years
then I went to freaking Teachers' College

another mistake!

like so many men I met
I left the surgeon behind
it was an interlude of

of love and laughter

7. *The TreehouseTreatment Centre – Guelph,*

All sins tend to be addictive,
and the terminal point of addiction is damnation.
  – W.H. Auden

I had spent the previous years
working hard on an English degree
then working even harder to get through

bloody Teachers' College

the stress of being sane and sober
and studying constantly
wore me down and I was ready for a

VERY BIG DRINK

Annie was performing in NYC and was on the bill with Blondie
I met her and she was great – books, music and booze –
were my escape

because of Annie, a world-famous singer,
I managed to meet Lou Reed, Todd Rundgren
Elvis Costello, Peter Gabriel, Sting, Bono, Marianne Faithfull
Beck, Leonard Cohen, and best of all

Nick Cave…twice.

back in real life
my first teaching job was a kindergarten class
it is the most stressful job one can have –

I was babysitting thirty little four and five year olds

utter chaos which started at 9 a.m.

just getting them into
the class and sitting down in a circle
was enough for me

it got so bad that I went to my doctor
reminded him stress mechanisms damaged
asked for a prescription for Valium

Valium is a tranquillizer
"mothers little helper"
extremely addictive

two weeks later I had doubled
the original dose
had a raging malignant tolerance

taking it each morning
just to get through the day
soon at the maximum dose and
feeling I still needed more

ten pills of 10 mg each meant
I was teaching and taking
100 mg of Valium daily

I tried to wean myself off but it was impossible
because I didn't seem to be able to
function on anything less

as soon as the school year finished
I checked myself into a private
hospital in Guelph, Ontario

once again, there I was —
institutionalized as a result of
my addictions

the Treehouse was a new place in an old building
many people in many programs
throughout the hospital

the addictions unit
the anxiety and depression unit
the post-traumatic stress program
the eating disorder clinic
the full-out crazy program

I knew Valium would be the most difficult drug to stop
but I wasn't aware of just how badly the place was run
the entire staff were people in recovery

the Director on a drunk!

they seemed soulless
without an ounce of compassion
I didn't stand a chance

things seemed not right
I was not assigned a doctor or a nurse
when everyone else had their own counsellors

one week in, one of the night staff said my nurse was Barb
Barb would walk past me in the hallway and glower
it was crazy — she was *crazy*!

I would see the other patients huddled into nooks
with their nurses in the evening and I would wonder
what was wrong with me and what was wrong with them?

one day a man arrived
pushing a wheelchair
down the corridor

my new roommate was being wheeled in
Sandy was in bad shape, a heroin addict
I felt terrible for her

she had arrived at the Treehouse
without being detoxed first
which was common practice

she lay in the bed next to me
sweating and groaning and crying for help –
to no avail

the nurses, those bitches, refused to alleviate her suffering
they seemed immune to her pleas
I would trudge up to the nurse's station

ask for an aspirin for Sandy
which they would hand over grudgingly
no one bothered to check on her

she couldn't take it
she left and
she died

the following week

I cried even more.

The first time I saw Rick

Epilogue – Love Is a Drug

Where you used to be, there is a hole in the world, which I find myself constantly walking around in the daytime, and falling in at night. I miss you like hell.
    – Edna St. Vincent Millay

'love one love one lost'

I first saw him
from atop
a Ferris wheel

he was standing below
with a group
of people I knew

he had long, black, curly hair
when everyone else
had short hair

he was the first
really beautiful
man I had ever seen

it was a cool fall evening
he was wearing a
black, fur coat

something told me
I had to meet him.
I noticed he was the centre of his friends' attention –

so arresting: sharp features, a little gap in his teeth
I asked his friend if I could meet him
three months later, I got an introduction

I went to a bar he always frequented
an oompah-pah tavern – men dressed in lederhosen
accordions, trombone, tuba and base

playing high-slapping German tunes

we went out
we fell in love
we were transcendent together

I had heard rumours about his
gorgeous Russian ex-girlfriend
it was always on my mind

I was constantly afraid she
would want him back...so insecure
we went out for a year and

became engaged
on Valentine's Day
my birthday

two weeks later the accident happened
no one knew of our engagement
a few months before, I was in grade thirteen

needed two courses to complete high school
still hating school, those awful
heavy, wool uniforms

I quit and went to night school
instead of getting up early for classes
I had no constraints

in a sense, I lived alone

my family right there, still on the periphery
I could not tell them anything
without the finger of blame pointing

straight at my heart

The Horror

There is no pain so great as the memory of joy in present grief.
— Aeschylus

A lethal winter evening after night school
Rick came to pick me up
he was driving a friend's old car

some kind of Mustang hatchback
spooky-looking death car
he lived in the country with his parents

we decided to drive out to his place
it was ten o'clock at night
I was eating peanuts

we pulled over and parked
somewhere down a dark road
no houses, no people

a starless, eerie night
cow paths in our headlights
white fences small lanes

an American wind
blowing south from
Detroit

we sat and we laughed
our future ahead
secure in the knowledge

of each others' hearts
listening to Bob Dylan
we both sang along

so young and so happy
my ring felt
like home

there were holes in the floorboard
the gas blowing in through the backseat
we had no idea — no time to get out

no reason to worry
no reason to hurry
no memory at all

started to feel sick
woozy — my stomach upset
the dashboard lights on

Rick was smiling and promising kids
we talked of their names
and order of birth

my head against the window
such alarming fatigue
Rick asked what was wrong

I just felt so sick
he held onto my hand
asked me to rest

woke up four days later out of a coma
no memory of pain nor needing to breathe
my eyes sealed shut I could not see

oozing sores all over my head
I lay in a bed but wasn't sure where
light in the intensive care unit was low

silence was sick
I knew something terrible had happened as
I slipped back down into death

I came to in blackness – this time
could hear someone crying at the end of my bed
I said, "Where's Rick?"

I didn't ask
what happened, just
"Where's Rick?"

my dad said he was in another hospital
he didn't tell me he had died
that he'd been waked and buried

my next memory was of someone
wheeling me in and out of elevators
on my way to the psychiatric unit

thought we had tried to commit suicide

carbon monoxide had stole through the holes
silently stealing his beautiful breath
silently stealing our baby for death

helluva time trying to convince
the doctors of an accident
not suicide

I could not I would not eat
lost fifteen pounds that terrible week
the psych ward for suicide attempts

Metropolitan Hospital

beginning to be able to open my eyes
was in a ward next to the nurse's station
with two other women

they sent Fr. Brunette
to tell me Rick had died
but I already knew

he was *gone*.

the priest told me of the funeral
Rick was buried at
Heavenly Rest

carbon monoxide poisoning takes four hours
to affect brain damage, five hours to kill
the skin turns cherry red

a farmer got worried when he saw the car parked
and called the police who called an ambulance
the next day at 4 p.m.

they found Rick dead
me curled in a ball
under the dashboard, unconscious

nineteen hours living beside him dying

I had a picture of Rick, a little photo booth
picture, blown up and hung above my bed
lying there in shock my first night home

someone touched the side of my face and said

"It's okay."

I know it was him

but it wasn't okay, nothing was
nothing ever would be
my whole family embarrassed and ashamed

they worried about their reputation
nothing else
brought shame on their heads, couldn't forgive
there wouldn't be any psychological help.

told me to get it together
I was starting
university in September

for them, the accident was an
everlasting, shocking disgrace
with which they couldn't cope

it became my nightmare
the worst of it started when I began classes
passing a group of students hearing,

"There's the girl who was found in a car. Her boyfriend died."

branded with shame

walked around campus feeling
everyone staring
picturing us dying alone in that car

numb and trying to wrap my mind around Rick's death
no closure no funeral
the last time I had seen him, he was laughing

for the next ten years, it was incredibly
difficult to understand what had
happened to us

hung out with a girl I knew
drank coffee and talked at the doughnut shop
that was the extent of my therapy at the time

people were afraid to be around me
to approach me
didn't know what to say

that's when I started

drinking.

I realize now you can't blame it on one thing – but it does
start somewhere and this is where it began for me

Dave Dixon, Rick's friend
asked me to come to the pub
I'd sit with my head down, try not to cry

people were dancing and I'd think,

Don't you know that life is misery?
People die
and you never ever
see them again.

a few weeks later I went back to the pub
the fourth beer was sorcery
booze eased my pain

I lived all that night and most of the next day
I've never understood how I survived nineteen hours

Why did I live and Rick didn't?

all the days since have posed that existential question:

What was the meaning of it all?

Why was I saved?

Should I even be asking these questions?

in the years that followed, I would be given
mouth-to-mouth resuscitation
in a hotel room in New York City

fall at a film festival party and destroy my front teeth
wake up in hospitals or stranger places
lose every friend I ever had
and man, end up in the drunk tank thrice!

so many times I should have died
I have always had this feeling that it wasn't just God
It was Rick and other family members that had gone before

something out there kept me from death
and I've lived and have a loving son and he is all that I need
I find some peace sometimes. If I had not had Kevin,
I would be dead.

somehow, I had to face people and figure out
a way forward
before, I was just trying to have a good time when I drank
now drinking had become the pivotal moment

I was desperately trying to escape

my drinking had turned *deadly.*

The Stories…

Panic

Dr. Walker asked me to stop by his office later that week. It seemed I might have a few more problems than originally discussed. Dr. Walker turned to me and said very softly, *"I don't want to frighten you, Jet, but you're showing signs of panic disorder, as well. You fainted yesterday and you weren't able to breathe, nor talk and the nurses checked your vitals and gave you CPR."*

"Oh no! Panic attacks. Now what?"

"Medication, of course," he said hopefully. *"A drug called Prozac."*

"I don't understand. Why do I need an anti-depressant?"

"Because of what happened to you. We can't believe you've not given up. I know you lost your fiancé Rick, your unborn child, your dad, your beloved sister Gail, your godson Mike, your oldest brother Terry, your best friend Stevie was murdered and your Mom died a long and painful death. With everything happening one after another, you haven't been able to process your grief and maybe these pills might help. Prozac has helped many people before you. The panic attack was caused by unre-

solved fear and grief. Once you're stabilized, we can begin the process of healing. You need to grieve and experience your pain so that you can get beyond it. We need to bring that pain out and get rid of it. Alcohol and drugs have drowned your sorrows, but it's there inside you. You are very strong to have withstood the terrible emotional pain you live with. We can treat you but not the Acquired Brain Injury you suffered in the accident. Your stress mechanisms have been damaged slightly and you've been self-medicating all these years. You can go home today and I'll treat you as an out-patient."

Looking back, friends would look at me with astonishment;

"You're still alive!"

I wasn't so sure. Was this depression? I mean, did I ever feel good – really happy, that pure bliss feeling – like when Kevin was born or the time I won that viciously hard tennis tournament, when I whumped that girl from Russia?

Now, that was euphoria.

Almost as good as drugs.

Locomotion

I told Mary that I didn't want to hitchhike all the way to Banff that late at night. I mean it was at least, a two-hour trip and we were a pair of unaccompanied young females, and that a Barbie-type scenario, did not make. Even I knew that, and it was generally agreed that I had no sense whatsoever.

So, there we were, thumbs out and long hair flowing in the dark autumn wind. Inevitably a car stopped within seconds and backed up, just a little too eager for me. But hey, who cares when you're young and witless? Three men peered through the grimy windows expectantly and I guess we passed muster because the doors swung open. We jumped in the car and roared off on the greatest misadventure of my life.

The three men were in varying degrees of disarray – not that Mary noticed. There was an older gentleman who called himself Mike, but the other two guys kept calling him Don, which I found slightly disconcerting. He was in his fifties, maybe, and I couldn't help but wonder what he was doing with these two sinister-looking brutes. Neither one of them looked in too good of shape.

When we finally reached Banff unmolested, I wanted to go back to our place pronto, but Mike/Don insisted that we go to the Banff Springs Hotel, where he had rented a suite with promises of champagne, caviar and wild abandon. I was not in the mood, not being particularly attracted to any one of these desperadoes, but to my dismay, Mary had somehow developed a serious interest in Mike/Don. It was completely unimaginable to me, but who was I to cast stones?

She begged and pleaded and even offered to pay me, if only I would please, please, go to the party with her – she would not go alone, nice girls that we were. She wanted to get to know this guy with the big mouth and lots of money (or so he said). I was becoming very apprehensive.

So now we're at this wild, crazy party and this Mike character really had rented a huge suite at the Banff Springs Hotel. (If you've ever been there you know what I'm talking about. Big bucks and lots of 'em.)

There were tables loaded with delicacies and booze everywhere, with people coming out of the woodwork. I met a woman named Margie from New York City and much to my surprise, she too had joined the worship cult of this creep.

I should mention why I was so leery of this man. He said his name was Michael Rutherford Jr. (don't you know), celebrated author of *Five Easy Pieces* and that he lived on Long Island, New York. He carried a dubious-looking black briefcase, chained to his wrist everywhere he went, even to the bathroom. I couldn't help but wonder whether he was carrying some kind of weapon in there. God, so jaded, at the ripe old age of twenty.

In the meantime, I'm still trying to deal with Mary, who at this point in the evening is ready to bear this man's child. I mean, have a little pride, why don't ya? The guy was grotesque.

Soon he began making suggestions that were so absurd and so absolutely out of this world that even now, I cringe. He wanted to take everyone to San Francisco. Now. In private planes. He would rent them.

With the aid of Huxley's favourite drug and against every lesson I'd ever learned in my short life, I got caught up. I still had grave misgivings about this mysterious stranger, but under the influence, the brainwashing had begun.

Mary began to launch an all-out attempt to convince me, to drive to the airport in Calgary with these miscreants and fly off in chartered Cessnas in the middle of the night, to God knows where. It's so maniacal, I do it. She bails out just as I climb into the car. On the way out of the hotel, Mr. Rutherford asks a young bellhop and a woman who worked at the front desk along for the ride. They both quit their jobs on the spot and away we go.

All the way to the airport I keep changing my mind. I know that I can't possibly fly down to the States with this madman without something macabre happening. To me. I try to get out at the first gas station we stop at and hide in the bathroom, but again, I'm dissuaded. I'm told I'm a wimp and they ask me if I'll spend the rest of my life dodging such incredible opportunities.

Finally, we arrive at the airport. It's 4 a.m when he disappears into the customs office. The next thing I know, I'm flying over the Rocky Mountains, the four of us in one plane and the rest in another. By this time, Mr. Michael Rutherford Jr. has picked up on my deep and abiding doubts, and I get the feeling he's none too pleased. He watches me all the time, which creates such a feeling of alarm within me that I can hardly contain my panic.

We reach Billings, Montana, a couple hours later. It strikes me as being awfully suspicious, that we have no problem entering the States. Yet another mysterious development, which I find troublesome, since here we are, crossing an international border in the early hours of the morning and the customs officers have no interest in us whatsoever. Two members of our party strongly resemble homicidal drug addicts and still, we sail right through as if we were Mother Theresa and entourage. They don't ask for our passports.

The first thing we do is get hotel rooms and I don't like the idea of having to share a room with Mike/Don. He very gallantly rents a room "just for the ladies" and picks the lucky little bellhop to bunk with him. The other guys get the last room. Off we go to our respective rooms and it seems like just a few minutes elapse before we hear loud thumps that seem to be emanating from the room next door, occupied by none other than Mike and the young bellhop.

It's now some eight hours since we've left the relative sanity of

Canada and there's beginning to be rumblings within the ranks. It seems not everyone is feeling quite so cocky the next morning.

I've made friends with the two homicidal drug addicts (of course) and we three seem to be a little saner than the rest. Stan and Greg begin to share my concern that all is not well in paradise, and that old Mike/Don may have a different agenda up his long, black sleeve.

We secretly convene at the local saloon. By this time, we've agreed that something is definitely not right with Michael Rutherford Jr. What's with the briefcase and those loud bumps in the night? Is he some kind of sicko fetish guy or something even too terrible to contemplate? Why does he keep yapping on and on about his friendship with the Kennedys? Why does he keep telling us that he has pictures of that poor Kennedy kid who had his leg cut off? Now that's gruesome!

The next day we meet in the restaurant and Mike and his briefcase host a small soiree featuring bottles of pink champagne, "for the ladies." We're talking 9 a.m here. Soon he begins a long, involved saga about the death of his wife in the fires of San Francisco, which to my untrained ear seems to be about a century off. As he becomes more and more loquacious, he begins to boast about his very close personal relationship with Teddy Kennedy. Well, now I've heard it all. It's all getting a bit too much. First of all, this guy looks like Anthony Hopkins in *Silence of the Lambs* and secondly, why is he hauling all of us around in private planes and spending so much money, if he doesn't have some dark, grim intentions?

That day, we fly to Jackson Hole, Wyoming – a famous ski resort for the very rich and just happens to be inaccessible by public transport. The town itself is laid out like some old West ghost town, with wooden boardwalks and hitching posts and all the doors to the different establishments swing in. Nobody's around because it's October and the fat cats have yet to arrive.

Each day I wake up a little more neurotic than the day before and soon, I'm making frenzied phone calls to my boyfriend back home, who happens to be a journalist and who tells me in no uncertain terms to get the hell out of there fast. In the meantime, he decides to trace the infamous Michael Rutherford Jr. and find out if I am travelling with an impostor. He calls back that evening and in a voice filled with terror, informs me that he has, in fact, spoken to the real Mr. Rutherford, not ten minutes ago, at his home on Long Island. Furthermore, he has divulged the whole sordid tale to my parents, who are frantically calling the RCMP to come to Wyoming to rescue me. It feels as if things are getting dangerously close to some terrible finale.

I organize an emergency meeting in our room and tell everyone I was right all along (I make sure to include this fact first), and that dear old Mike is not the man he appears to be. Suddenly, we notice the briefcase hidden behind a chair. He had gone out for cigarettes three hours before and for some reason, had neglected to chain it to his wrist. I want to open that briefcase. I need to open that briefcase, I can't stand it any longer. Before we can break into it, there's a loud banging at the door.

We're all so freaked out, nobody will open it. At last, Stan gets up and opens the door. A huge police officer with a Smokey the Bear hat fills the door.

In a loud, booming voice, he demands to know whether we recognize the suspect in the squad car. We peek through the curtains and lo and behold, if it isn't Mike/Don sitting in the back seat, with a shotgun pointed at his head.

The big cop informs us that the perp is under arrest for something he declines to divulge. After they screech away, we try desperately to jimmy the locked briefcase. It finally pops open and unbelievably, there it is – a photograph of Teddy Kennedy and his son with Mr. Mike/Don himself. Astonishment!

We are flabbergasted. Why did the cops have a gun at his head? That seemed a little severe. Unless? What crime had he committed? Who the hell was he? One thing was certain: in the unlikely event he was released that night, he must not – I repeated, not be allowed back into our room to get the case unless there was a cop standing beside him. He was obviously some kind of dangerous psychopath if the cops had to actually hold a gun to his head. We fell into an uneasy sleep late that night after his groupies assured the rest of us that no way would they open that door.

I awoke to him, sitting on my bed, inches from my face, demanding to know why, why, why I had never liked him. He accused me of calling the cops on him. He was crying, holding a butter knife in his hand and tapping it against my thigh. I thought this was it – I was dead. Very soon. After the longest 10 minutes I've ever had the displeasure to endure, he abruptly jumped up and ran out of the room, briefcase in hand.

The women were screaming, "Michael, Michael, don't go." I couldn't believe them. Were they fucking nuts? I was just about murdered (albeit with a butter knife) and these crazed women wanted him to come back and "talk about it." I never did find out who opened the door that night to let him in, but I have my suspicions. So, there we were, stranded in Jackson Hole, Wyoming. I have a picture of all of us, standing outside the motel room, looking exceedingly pale. My poor mother wired me the money and I flew out later that day, returning to Banff.

Six months later, I got a call from the F.B.I. in Florida. They traced me to my parents' home somehow. I wondered how they'd gotten my name. They wanted to know if I knew a Michael Rutherford Jr. I said no.

Not the real one.

The Man Is Naked

Just after landing a teaching job at the Foothills Indoor Tennis Club in Calgary, I found a great place to live – an old, enfeebled Victorian house, complete with turrets and leaded glass windows. It was downtown, close to the club and the rent was an unbelievable 200 bucks a month for the ground-floor flat. Strange as it may seem, after paying the first months' rent, the landlord never came to collect the rent again, so I lived there for free.

From the aerie that was my bedroom, I could see through the ample glass of the French doors, the stone steps descending to a grove of trees, their arching bows, a leafy canopy shielding the sumptuous sanctuary of a lush garden. Such dense foliage cloaked the house allowing me to roam the grounds undetected. I was secure in the knowledge that I wasn't visible and more importantly, seen to be living there alone. Home from the tennis club by 2 p.m., I would slip into my bathing suit, head for my private Garden of Eden, set up my chaise longue in the sun, roll a joint, pour a glass of wine (or two), stretch out and listen to my favourite Motown soul, (ever hopeful that my freckled skin would somehow tan).

My customary peace was shattered one hot Friday afternoon by a loud knocking. I thought it must be the landlord because I had not told anyone of my exact location. I hurriedly threw a shirt over my bathing suit and hustled through to the front door, neglecting to look through the peephole. I swung the heavy door open and there stood

A Naked Man.

"Oh my God, Oh my God, Oh my God."

I screamed and slammed the door in his face, tore back through the house closing drapes, locking windows and making sure the French doors were bolted. Shaken, I made my way to the phone and called the police. I was frantic. Why was this guy standing on my front porch without a stitch? Had he just strolled down the street and happened to turn in at my house? He must have stashed his clothes in the bushes, knowing he would not be seen from the street.

I waited for the cops to come as I hastily downed another glass of wine. This could not be happening. It was just too bizarre.

A second knock! A squint through the lens of the peephole revealed two detectives. I opened the door gingerly. They asked me to step outside and began asking questions.

"What colour was his hair?" smirked the first detective.

"I really didn't get a good look at his hair."

"Well, what colour were his eyes?" they countered.

"I didn't get a good look at his eyes, either," I answered.

Snicker, snicker.

They began to look around the property and then advised me to get a friend to come and stay with me. I'd just moved to the city, didn't know anybody, and didn't have another place to stay.

The police assured me they would have a patrol car parked in front of my house and told me not to worry.

"Right," I thought. "The naked maniac is probably going to come back here in the middle of the night and murder me."

Their theory was that someone had been watching me from a high-rise apartment near my house and the appearance of my man was a one-off thing.

But not in my mind. The vision of my naked visitor haunted me night and day. I was sick with fear and the only relief I got came when I drank.

One morning I awoke to find that the leaded glass windows throughout the house had been cut out. Apparently leaded glass is rare and fetched good money.

Just about the time I began feeling a little safer, I decided to go camping with two girls I'd met through tennis. As we were leaving, I noticed a woman moving into the flat on the top floor of my house. She was very fair, had long blonde hair and freckles, and was about the same height and size as me but I was amazed – she looked just like me! It was strange that my doppelganger was now living above me and at the same time, I was pleased to have a neighbour upstairs. Life would be safe again.

When I got back to town from camping I took a cab home. As soon as we turned the corner to my block, I could smell smoke and saw the fire engines.

"What address did'ya want?" the cabbie asked me.

I could barely answer for fear it was my house that was burning. Sure enough, there it was, with no top half to the house left. The turrets were gone and it was now a square block of smouldering wood. I got out of the cab and nervously made my way toward the fireman standing before the front porch.

"I live here," I gulped. "What happened?"

One of the fireman told me not to worry as the bottom of the house had not caught fire. He took me into the house and showed me the streaks of black soot running up and down the inside walls.

He then took me to the top of the stairs. There was nothing left of the apartment. It was horrendous. My doppelganger had not been home when the fire was set. Later, I found out that two men had broken in and had soaked the walls and floors with gasoline and set the place alight.

She looked just like me.

Shovelling Shit

After living in a state of constant terror in the topless mansion and after losing my job as a tennis pro at the indoor club for drinking at my boss's wedding and getting wasted, my life began sliding inexorably downhill.

Somehow, I got a job in construction of all things and began working as a surveyor on a highway project outside of Calgary. I drove around in a truck with four men and was the designated plumb bob holder. I began to enjoy this job, as the guys I worked with were very nice and also, I had a crush on my friend Peter, who was from Windsor too.

I got the truck at lunchtime and went on a mission to find the most food, for the least money, which meant Taco Bell or Burger King.

I would arrive for work at 8 a.m. and proceed to go for breakfast, which lasted till 10 a.m. and meant eating bacon and eggs and drinking copious amounts of coffee. After having a fat-filled lunch, I would go home and eat large amounts of spaghetti before I went out to the only punk club in Calgary, the Calgarian. I was beginning to put on weight because I was eating junk all day and drinking draft beer at night in the bar. Soon I had put on twenty pounds and kept getting fatter and fatter and fatter.

I tried not to worry about it, because after all, I was out

west and no one could see me. Soon I was topped the scales at 150 pounds – which is a lot of weight when one is 5'4.

At a party one night I met two people who would become my new best friends and were, in fact, witness to my greasy slide down into the murky world of music and drugs.

The first was Michael, who insisted to anyone who would listen that he was from Vancouver, when in reality he had come from Ralph, Saskatchewan. He was a tiny little guy, a writer and a bloody good wit. We became instant friends as he was well read and we could talk (and drink) for hours about our favourite books.

My second friend was called Norma Jean. She had adopted a punk persona, complete with black hair, nails and clothes. She was an extremely talented painter and I adored her.

My western odyssey went from good to bad to worse. I'd made friends with a neighbor, who offered me a room in the house he rented, two doors away from where I lived, in the smokehouse.

I wanted out of that house so bad that I agreed to pay him 300 bucks a month, for the pleasure of renting a dank basement room, where I smoked lots of hash oil that winter, just to block the strangeness above.

Unfortunately, I had to walk through his bedroom to get to the door that led down to my dungeon. My new landlord had a prosthetic leg and would frequently ask me and Michael, if we wanted to see him take it off. He was strange, but nothing I thought I needed to be concerned about. His deviancy extended into the music he listened to. It was deafening, boisterous, irreverent death metal music and caused me to become even more desperate to get out of there and find somewhere safe.

Six months later, I was still living in his house of pain and fending him off. He was not overt, but the idea of my being with him made me ill and cast a pall over me every time I walked into that house.

The problem, though, was that I had been laid off from my construction job. It had ended in November, and that meant I had no dough to get out of this living arrangement.

It all came to a head one morning when I awoke to the disgusting smell of shit everywhere.

"What's going on?" I wondered and as I stepped out of my room, I was horrified to see what I saw. The entire basement was covered with a foot of slimy, wet shit. There was crap all the way over to the steps upstairs. Worse, I could hear him at the basement door yelling.

"You broke my toilet! You clean it up!"

It made no sense: That amount of waste couldn't have come from the toilet I used, which was situated right next to my room.

He stomped down the stairs and threw me a shovel and garbage bags. He was a formidable enemy and I knew not to argue or resist. Instead, I did what he asked. I donned my rubber boots and proceeded to shovel all that shit into garbage bags. I couldn't breathe...the smell was so bad.

I kept telling him that it must have been the toilets from the two upper apartments. There were three in total. It must have come down from the top, to the second floor where he was and into the basement toilet. But he didn't care, and simply stood at the top of the stairwell screaming "faster, faster."

I told him I needed to go to the store to buy more garbage bags and I escaped to the nearest bar. I called a friend named Art who had been on the construction job and he agreed to help me. We made plans for that very night. I began packing my books and clothes and prepared to sneak out in the middle of the night. Art picked me up at 4 a.m. and I was out of there. It took me a few weeks to find another place and by that time, I was heavily invested in the music scene and luckily, found a room with two singers who were fairly normal but by then; my drinking had spun out of control. I was spending my nights with Michael and Norma Jean at the Calgarian, listening to New Wave bands coming out of Vancouver. We drank, we danced and then we drank some more.

Things seemed all right in my world if I had a bottle of Silent Sam in the freezer and enough drugs to see me through but I sensed things were coming to an end in Calgary and I'd need to make plans to get the hell out of there and get back home, to Ontario.

The Homecoming

After spending a year and a half in Banff and Calgary, I was more than ready to go back home. I had a large problem though. I now weighed in at 180 pounds, which was 75 pounds heavier than when I left Windsor.

In an attempt to try to disguise my extremely heavy body, I would wear a large black suit coat everywhere I went. This presented another problem; it was now summertime and quite warm, and so, I could only comfortably leave the house after dark. My ensemble fit with the punks at night but looked very strange in the light of day.

Norma Jean and Michael decided to throw a party the night before I was to fly out. All the punks came out; the music was loud and in the absence of any kind of good sense, I decided to drop some acid, because I had always wondered what it would be like to fly, while flying high – a grievous mistake on my part and not a decision I would've made if I hadn't been drunk. My flight was scheduled to leave at 6 a.m. and I meant to party hard on my last night there.

I had bought a new dark suit coat, thinking it would disguise the ton of fat I was hauling around, as I was deeply ashamed of the fact that I had let myself go like that. A guy at the party drove a taxi and so it was decided that he and as many people as he could fit in the cab would drive me to the airport.

I made the flight just in time and as I was trying to fit my bulk down the narrow aisle, someone called my name.

"Jet, Jet – are you Jet Ryan?"

"Yes, yes I am," I gratefully answered the lady with a baby.

Her name was Sheila and she had been on the tennis team at university with me. She quickly arranged to have my seat changed, so that I could sit with her and her daughter on the long flight home.

As the plane rose through the pink sky of sunrise, I felt an odd taste at the back of my throat. "What have I done?" I thought. There was no backing out. I couldn't believe I had been so stupid and not thought ahead, to the fact that my family would be at the airport, awaiting my arrival. Panic set in and I could barely contain my terror. In desperation I told Sheila what I had taken and the reason why.

She scoffed at me and said, "Here, take a couple of these, it will calm you down and I'll order drinks too."

"It's 8 a.m. though," I said worriedly.

"We're on a plane, remember?" she laughed.

Sheila handed me two Valium and ordered a couple of drinks – Black Russians, to be precise. Pure alcohol and not something, for someone, in my state of mind.

On the phone with her the next day, she sadly recounted my bizarre arrival home. I had no memory of what had transpired and I was still feeling shaky.

According to her, I was functioning when the plane landed at its first stop in Winnipeg. I have a vague memory of wheeling the baby around the airport in her stroller.

Apparently, my entire family, including my dog, were at the airport that day, happily expecting to be joyously reunited with me.

They waited and waited and after at least ten minutes of the last passenger disembarking, they could hear sirens. To their horror, the ambulance crossed the tarmac and parked alongside the plane.

They saw the ambulance attendants carrying a gurney down the steps of the plane with a massive lump under the blanket. The fat, prodigal daughter returning from combat!

I awoke to a woman leaning over me asking if I wanted a drink.

"I don't think so," I quipped. "I've had enough."

"Water?" she asked again.

I realized that I recognized her from high school. That's one of the reasons I had left Windsor and why I had felt the need to escape. My drinking had become an embarrassment to my family and everyone I knew were witness to my fall from grace – the tennis prodigy turned addict. I hated the way people I knew saw me drunk and stoned again and again. They didn't know that I was sick and I didn't know either.

They released me from the hospital that night. Oh the shame! I went home and got out an old shirt of my dad's.

My mum and my sister called me downstairs to "talk." My sister looked at me and then at my mother. My mother looked at my sister and then at me. It was so ridiculous; the whole situation that all we could do was laugh, because that was better than crying.

Mr Sexy

As if you were fire from within.
The moon lives in the lining of your skin.
　　　– Pablo Neruda

For three years, I sat in the upstairs window of my apartment, watching the English guy who lived next door, drive up in his English sports car, wearing his English green leather jacket. I wonder now how I knew that he was English, because he looked a bit Slavic, like a young Marlon Brando. It's just not possible for a man to get any sexier than that. Green eyes, high cheekbones, full lips. He was part of a group of four guys who rented the house next door. I had made friends with one of them and he must've been the one who told me that Mr. Sexy was, indeed, from England.

One Saturday night, as I was walking home, I noticed they were having a party and I was invited in. I took one look at who was sitting on the front porch and when I saw him, I hurtled up the sidewalk and made a beeline straight for the porch where he was sitting. There was a blonde woman stretched languidly across him. My friend introduced us and that was it. I didn't want to stand there and gape, so I hastily said goodbye to my friend and went home.

I lived next door to a God!

The next morning, I got my tennis clothes together to take to the laundromat. I had a good job as tennis pro with the

Ontario Tennis Association, working at a club downtown. I didn't own a lot of tennis whites, so therefore, had to make the trip to the laundromat every Sunday morning, in preparation for the week ahead.

On my way up the street, I spotted my next-door Adonis walking toward me. As I passed him he looked up and I said hello. I thought it would be okay to greet him as I had officially met him the night before. I reached Queen Street, turned left and continued on my way. I stopped to look at the books in the window of the bookstore and that's when I realized Mr. Sexy was right behind me.

He told me later that he had thought I was waiting for him, but I was so very shy that I wouldn't have thought that he was following me. I had no self-confidence and no self-esteem whatsoever. It didn't matter how many people told me I was beautiful; I just couldn't believe it. My brothers and my dad had done a very good job of destroying every ounce of confidence I ever had.

I fell sadly in love that day and only now, years and years later, when I think of David, I don't cry. I loved him with every fibre of my being. He was everything I had always dreamed of. Not only was he physically beautiful, but he had a beautiful mind, a mixture of art and science. He had only been in Canada for three years, after studying in England and completing his degrees. He was smart, he was funny, and best of all, he loved me.

He followed me into the laundromat and I was very embarrassed having to throw my underwear and other unmentionables into the wash machine in front of him.

I had a pair of black pants that I wore constantly and David noticed that the hem was down.

"Shall I fix your slacks for you?" he asked in his sexy English accent.

"What?" I answered.

"I can sew and I'll hem them for you."

"Okay?" God – he could sew too!

When I got home from work the next day, I rushed upstairs, threw on a long T-shirt and prepared to lay back and relax. I was so happy to be out of the sun and back home. Suddenly, the doorbell rang. I went flying down the stairs, thinking it was my friend Cathy and I opened the door.

It was him, my English god! He had a big smile on his face and handed over my pants, telling me that I should check the hem to make sure the job was done right. I was shaking; I was so surprised to see him.

I tore back up the stairs and retrieved said pants out of the bag. I had no idea of what was coming next but it's probably one of the most glorious moments of my life. I was that affected.

I checked the pants and saw that he had done a wonderful job and as I was looking at the hem, I saw something white, maybe a white thread? I picked at it and realized that it was a tiny corner of a piece of white paper. I pulled on it and out came a long, tiny rectangle of paper that had been folded up many, many times to be able to place it in the hem.

Slowly, I unravelled it and sure enough, there was a note. The note said,

The way to a woman's heart is through her pants. Will you have dinner with me?

I howled with utter delight. This was brilliant. It was out-of-this world clever. In years to come, that moment will last forever. I will never forget the man who did that for me.

Game Over

I sat on my bed, swallowing whiskey and drinking pills, and realized that once in a while the improbable would happen, the unthinkable sometimes happened, and the unbearable did happen. I know I'm being bad, but I just can't help myself. I Just. Can't. Help. Myself.

I think of the last night I didn't go out with Stevie Cohen – my sweet, loving and crazy Jewish friend who I had known since we were eight-year-old kids winning tournaments together and hanging out at the tennis courts in Jackson Park, downtown Windsor.

Stevie Cohen was a dark, little sprite, full of mischief and laughter. His little, freckled face and black eyes danced with glee. The first time I met him, he was sitting with a group of his friends at the courts when I walked by. He called out:

Hey Jet! Did you know that Jewish guys are circumcised?

After I recovered from the shock and embarrassment I learned later that summer that Stevie was funny and we had a blast together. We were inseparable and would play tennis all day and late into the hot, summer nights.

Later, neither of us had dealt with life very well and we both fell head over heels in love with sex and drugs and rock'n'roll, which was a lot easier than hitting tennis balls and striving to keep my tennis ranking. We both lay our tennis racquets down and got our mojos working.

I moved to Toronto and he stayed in Windsor and decided to live on top of the store his dad owned. He was my go-to-guy when I hit Windsor, after months and months of being very good in Toronto. I had someone to take care of my son in Windsor and that was my passport to get wild.

Stevie and I had planned to go to Detroit one Tuesday night, because I was going back to Toronto the next day, but that presented a problem. There was never a night that Steve and I hung out in Detroit – or even when we stayed home in Windsor – for that matter, without calamity happening. Either he would leave me in Detroit, drunk and helpless at some bar, or we would go on a two-day binge in some small, greasy club off the beaten path, not far from Greektown.

The worst club was on Harper Street; crazy sweating people, the bright lights burning, we'd drink all night long and as much as we could and consume as many drugs as possible, rendering us catatonic. We liked it like that, but my family held their collective breath until I would stagger home the next morning.

Somehow my sister Gail got wind of my impending visit with Steve and she phoned and implored, "Please, just this once Jet...Please don't go out with Stevie tonight!"

I quickly assured her, then promptly called Stevie and made plans to meet at 7:30 on Erie Street.

I looked at my baby boy, lying on the bed, smiling at me and I decided that this night, this time, I would do what my sister asked and not see Steve.

We loved Detroit. We loved the music, the bars and the gritty streets, but most of all we loved to escape, and there was not a feeling in the world that could compare to the giddy freedom we felt, hitting those American freeways, careening towards our next high. Escape Windsor, escape the people we knew, and most importantly...escape ourselves.

Stevie and I were very much alike in that respect, although he did have a head start on me. He was treated for heroin addiction at a treatment centre in California before I had even heard the word "marijuana" and now he was back in Windsor, the scourge of the Jewish community, that he was so reluctantly a part of. We left all the crap behind when we crossed the border and landed headfirst into the teeming, intoxicating streets of Detroit.

Two weeks later, my mother phoned me crying. Stevie had been murdered on the very night I had cancelled on him. Two young psychopaths, stoned on cocaine, had stabbed my Stevie sixty-three times in the chest. The police thought it was a gunshot wound.

He was dead. They had found him sitting in the chair where I always sat whenever I was at his place, only that night I was safe at home.

My family had not wanted me to know; they didn't think I'd be able to deal with yet another death. And they were right. I couldn't.

Steve was dead and I might as well have been. It was only later I knew that his death had become my beginning.

Epiphany

It is never too late to be what you might have been.
  — George Elliot

Dishevelled and distraught, I made my way down A Street, looking for the bus stop. Luckily, I still had a bit of change left, enough for the fare. The waiting was painful; the rays of the rising sun, glancing off the mirrored office towers like shards of broken glass, slicing the truth into my beat-up brain. I cursed myself for not having my sunglasses with me, but then again, why would I have needed them?

When the bus finally came, I clambered on in my skin-tight evening dress under the sober-eyed scrutiny of passengers, on their way to work. Down the aisle I strode, leaving a wake of imagined whispers behind me. I took a seat at the very back berating myself, stop after stop. And then she got on.

I watched her walk down the aisle, heading straight for me. She sat down next to me, smiled and said in a beautiful Irish brogue, "Hi. I'm Sharon. I just got here a couple of months ago from Dublin. I love what you're wearing."

We immediately started to chat up a storm; you know the way that can happen. I told her I'd been at a party all night and that I had the hangover from hell. The last thing I could remember was holding a bottle of wine in each hand while I shakily made my way towards a leather couch, where I had apparently stayed for the next eight hours, deep in another blackout. Now I was on my way home, to be confronted by my boyfriend who would be angrily waiting for me on yet another leather couch.

Sharon hugged me and said, "Ah, you poor, wee thing. It's in our blood, they say. You're Irish through and through."

At that point, I perked right up, seized the moment and confided the fact that I was a direct descendent of the first King of Ireland. I rarely get the chance to tell this to anyone and it seemed like the perfect opportunity for some much needed admiration.

"Aren't we all, sweetie?" Sharon laughed. "Now, why don't you meet me tonight at an AA meeting? There's a good group in the basement of the church at the corner of Washington and Cass. There'll be lots of good-looking lads to take your mind off the drink. Be there by eight." With that, she gave me her phone number and away she went.

Looking out the window, I realized with trepidation that I was approaching my neighbourhood. I didn't enjoy slinking down the street, past all the shopkeepers who had seen it all before. To my everlasting shame, the guy across the street had found me, slumped in his doorway, unable to get up and get home. Ever the lady!

With high heels in hand, I stole up the stairs, hoping my boyfriend wouldn't be home. Loudly, I heard him call my name as I ran as fast as could for the shelter of the bathroom, where I could lock the door. I tore off my dingy, black dress and my torn, black tights, and jumped into the tub, hoping the hot, soapy water would wash my sins away. As the steam rose around me, I slunk down low in the bath, *praying for absolution*.

Author Bio Note

Bridget Ryan was born and raised in Windsor, Ontario across the river from Detroit. Her teenage years saw the glory days of a booming automotive industry, the blossoming alternative Pop culture and the lure of Motown, Rock 'n' Roll and Punk Rock.

Born last in a large Irish Catholic family, she excelled in most sports, but found comfort in the solitude of tennis and quickly achieved ranking.

Through her teens, the suffocation of prim Windsor forced her gang of friends to cross over to 'Murder City' to check out the hottest clubs and on many occasions, were rewarded with sightings of The Rolling Stones, Patti Smith, and The Ramones. From a very young age, her attraction to literature bloomed under the tutelage of some of America's greatest writers: Salinger, Fitzgerald, and Kerouac.

Bridget completed a Bachelor of Arts in English Literature with a minor in Creative Writing at York University in Toronto, Ontario and then went on to attain a Bachelor of Education degree, also from York.

Bridget has worked as a Librarian, a Physical Education Teacher and as a Literacy Teacher at a school board in Toronto, Ontario.

Her passion for live music, poetry and literature have led her on many a harrowing soul searching trips. Her memoir, *Bitches With Problems*, is a collection of stories culled from her boisterous travels through addiction, asylums, death and back again.

www.ingramcontent.com/pod-product-compliance
Lightning Source LLC
LaVergne TN
LVHW012105070526
838202LV00056B/5637